The Lord's Prayer
An Eastern Perspective

The Lord's Prayer
An Eastern Perspective

by
Kwan-Yuk C. Sit

薛羅君鈺

STEINERBOOKS

Kwan-Yuk C. Sit (薛羅君鈺)
Riverdale, N. Y.
USA

Library of Congress Cataloging-in-Publication Data

Sit, Kwan-Yuk C.
   The Lord's prayer : an Eastern perspective / Kwan-Yuk C. Sit
     p. cm.
   Includes bibliographical references (p.   ) and index.
   ISBN 978-0-88010-596-5
   1. Lord's prayer—Criticism, interpretation, etc. 2. Asia—Religion.
3. Philosophy, Asian. 4. Christianity and other religions. 5. Spiritual
life. I. Title.
   BV230.S46 2008
   226.9'606—dc22

                                                    2008033649

Production Editor: William Sit.
The Lord's Prayer, in Chinese, calligraphed by Kit-Keung Kan (靳杰强).
Copyright ©2007 by Kit-Keung Kan.
(reproductions appearing on cover, and inside with dedication)

Copyright ©2008 Kwan-Yuk C. Sit

Published by SteinerBooks
610 Main Street, Great Barrington, MA 01230
www.steinerbooks.org

Printed in the United States of America
9 8 7 6 5 4 3 2 1

Table of Contents

Notes

Romanization

In this book, many Eastern names are romanized. Names of Chinese origin may be romanized under different systems, but following Chinese tradition, will be written with family name first, then given name(s). For well-known names such as Lao Tzu and Confucius, the Wade-Giles system is used. For Chinese names or terms less familiar to the general public in the West, the pinyin system is favored and their Chinese originals are provided in the Index.

The Bible

All quotes from *The Bible* in this book are taken from *The Holy Bible*, Revised Standard Version, Catholic Edition, Dom Bernard Orchard and Revd. R. C. Fuller eds., Catholic Truth Society, London, 1966.

Text of
The Lord's Prayer

Our Father who art in heaven,

Hallowed be thy name,

Thy kingdom come,

Thy will be done on earth as in heaven.

Give us this day our daily bread,

And forgive us our trespasses

As we forgive those who trespass against us.

Lead us not into temptation, but deliver us from evil.

For thine is the kingdom, the power,

And the glory, forever and ever.

Amen.

This version is modified from the one in *The Son of Man* by Andrew Harvey [32, p. 222].

The Lord's Prayer in Chinese
with a dedication to the author
(Calligraphy by Kit-Keung KAN).

Acknowledgements

This book project thrived on the kindness and generosity of many helping hands. Anyone who has written a book understands the immeasurable and invaluable help from teachers and friends, past and present. It is never a solo project.

My first and foremost thanks go to Edward R. Smith, who corresponded with me and inspired me to take on this project. He also graciously read an early draft of the whole manuscript, gave valuable suggestions, and maintained his interest in its progress. I am overwhelmed by the enthusiasm he and his son Mark demonstrated after reading the manuscript. It was through Mark's effort that the speedy publication of this book by SteinerBooks was facilitated. It was my pleasure to work with the staff at SteinerBooks. I thank especially Mary Giddens for her meticulous attention to details, and William Jensen for his help in designing the cover.

To Michael Barnsley, I owe the beautiful illustrations on the Mandelbrot and Julia sets. His kind permission to reproduce them is greatly appreciated.

It is very gratifying to have many relatives and friends, in particular Anna CHAN, Yuen-Han KAN, Yuk-Ching KWAN, and Helena SIT, who show their keen interest in my project. Thanks are due to Ka-Lai Lo, Man-Wai So, Po-Ching Wong, and Ho Wong, who read the manuscript and gave useful feedback. I would like to express my special appreciation to Matthew Chan for his many uplifting remarks and encouragement, to Rufus Ho for his humorous critique in the tone of Confucius, and to Lester Lee for his insightful, meticulous, and expert comments, editorial corrections, and suggestions.

The dedication in Chinese calligraphy by Kit-Keung Kan of Bethesda, Maryland aesthetically enlivens the cover of the book and I am very much honored by his generosity.

It is my great fortune that my sister Alice and my son Eugene patiently acted as sounding boards allowing me to brainstorm with them many of my early ideas. Thanks are due to my sister-in-law Ying Lo for suggesting ways to write a preface. No words can express my deep gratitude to my husband William, who spent months with me to refine the narratives of the manuscript and took up voluntary duties as editor, indexer, graphics illustrator, and typesetter.

To all who have contributed to make this book a reality, whether explicitly mentioned above or not, I would like to express my deep gratitude: a million thanks. May the knowledge that someone will find this monograph consoling be the reward of their contributions.

Preface

This book opens the door to Eastern religious and cultural practices in an attempt to shed light on the teachings implicit in *The Lord's Prayer*. It uses simple analogies and inspiring anecdotes to unveil seemingly subtle and obscure Eastern concepts. It paves a path for Self-realization along the trail of *The Lord's Prayer*, merging the precious teachings of Eastern and Western masters from the Buddha, Confucius, Lao Tzu, Mother Teresa, The Dalai Lama, and others. It is written for people who seek inspiration to enrich their lives, who desire greater mastery of Eastern philosophy, and who value information on practical spirituality.

My first encounter with *The Lord's Prayer* took place in junior high school when I studied the Catholic Catechism. After baptism, I mainly said *The Lord's Prayer* in a hurry as a confession penance. During college days I was stirred by the urge to unravel the mystery of human existence. I met a kind and open-minded Jesuit priest at a retreat and thereafter frequently consulted him for guidance for about a year. However, feeling frustrated that the church doctrines seemed unable to help me unlock that mystery, I stopped going to church and subsequently did not say *The Lord's Prayer* or any prayer for a long time.

I have read widely to broaden my perspectives on life and was intrigued to learn that many deeply spiritual personalities and mystics said *The Lord's Prayer* regularly. In *The Way of Perfection* [72, p. 105], St. Teresa of Avila (1515–1582) exhorts her nuns to use *The Lord's Prayer* as a guide for a perfect life of prayer in the convent. Sharing with them her profound insights as a contemplative, she advises them to say *The Lord's Prayer* slowly so as to ponder its meanings in depth. She suggests to them:

> It would be a good idea for us to imagine that He [Jesus] has taught this prayer to each one of us individually and that He is continually teaching it to us.

Rudolf Steiner (1861–1925), a noted spiritual teacher, said *The Lord's Prayer* consistently at three o'clock every afternoon. He encouraged his students to repeat daily some simple activities, especially non-essential ones such as watering a plant or reciting a poem in reverse. He explained that fostering such a habit would develop self-discipline and even esoteric abilities. In *The Son of Man* [32, pp. 222–230], Andrew Harvey (b. 1952), a dedicated spiritual seeker, illustrates a systematic way to contemplate *The Lord's Prayer* based on the practices of St. Teresa and other Christian mystics. Thanks to their teachings, I have greatly expanded my horizon in appreciating *The Lord's Prayer*.

My reading list also includes books on health and related topics. Dr. Herbert Benson (b. 1935), an American cardiologist who pioneered his research on the mind-body relation, reported in 1975 in *The Relaxation Response* [3] the amazing effects of transcendental meditation on the body. Since then, many studies have been conducted that reaffirm the benefits of meditation for both the body and the mind. Some results even claim that one hour of deep meditation is more effective than four hours of sleep for reinvigorating our being. It is widely believed that the practice would help a person live holistically and peacefully.

Except for occasional insomnia, I do not have any critical health problems. However, I am extremely impatient and get upset easily. After a sleepless night, I often become more irritable. In my preteen days I lost my temper so often that one of my uncles enjoyed teasing me by giving me the nickname "Cross Ginger." Gingers, especially mature and old gingers, are very hot to the palate. He might have called me "Old Ginger" but for my then young age. Since I became cross so easily, he labeled me "Cross Ginger" instead. My husband, reacting to my impatience, once exclaimed teasingly, "You are more than Type A. You are Type Triple A!" Some students also complained that I became impatient when they wanted me to explain some simple concept over again. Occasionally a student would whisper, "Gee, she is upset." I might not have been that upset by the circumstances, but their remarks really upset me!

I wanted to be more patient and wondered if the practice of meditation would help me be less agitated. Would its calming power be so effective that I would become as undisturbed as the sage who, even if Tai Shan— the First Mountain of China— crumbled in front of him, would not stir an iota?

I began to fantasize that if I ever take up the practice, I would aim at meditating for at least two hours at a time so that the practice might free me from the tyranny of sleep and would allow me extra time to pursue more interests. So one day I embarked on the practice of meditation. The moment chosen to start the practice was probably not an auspicious one. I seemed to be sitting on a blanket of needles. The ten-minute meditation session as suggested for beginners felt like eternity to me. I kept peeking at the clock. My mind was racing like a wild horse or poking around like a curious monkey.

One time I tried sitting cross-legged on the floor and seemed to be able to quiet my mind a little and stayed in the position longer. I cherished this tiny improvement and imagined this might be the right way for me. But in reality the apparent success was short-lived. Soon after, I dreamt that two monkeys on the ceiling kept poking at me for fun with their hands while I was taking a shower. The scenario of this dream befits the metaphor that the mind acts like a monkey that can never be still. I knew then I was far from improving.

Hoping that books on meditation would guide me to success, I read whatever came my way. I practiced off and on for a number of years without any progress. Before completely abandoning the practice after many unfruitful attempts, I decided to experiment with contemplating *The Lord's Prayer*, expecting this alternative approach to practice meditation would yield positive results. I reasoned that even if this method should turn out to be unsuccessful, it would be better to have my mind run wild on the Lord's words than to have it distracted by a mischievous monkey show! I used to say *The Lord's Prayer* very rapidly in Chinese; perhaps saying it in English would slow me down and allow me to uncover some of its special meanings.

There are many versions of *The Lord's Prayer* and Harvey suggests picking a version that one likes. Having no particular preference I simply based mine on the one in Harvey's book (see p. vii) and followed his example of contemplation. I pondered each clause to learn what significance it would have for me. Over a span of several months I gained a perspective of *The Lord's Prayer* that was refreshing and nurturing for my well-being. Since then I have been regularly contemplating *The Lord's Prayer* and this practice keeps deepening my appreciation of the hidden messages in it.

There are of course different ways to interpret *The Lord's Prayer*. For example, Dan Campbell (1908–1974), in *Edgar*

Cayce on the Power of Colors, Stones, and Crystals [4, p. 107], explains how to associate key words of *The Lord's Prayer* with the seven glands. Edward R. Smith (b. 1932), in *The Burning Bush* [60, pp. 436–437], reproduces a seven-pointed schematic of *The Lord's Prayer* by which Steiner illustrates how the seven petitions in *The Lord's Prayer* address the seven components of the human being.

With this little monograph, I am sharing with you my musings on *The Lord's Prayer*. I simply follow St. Teresa or Harvey's approach. I will neither relate *The Lord's Prayer* to any particular part of the body nor consider the lines in *The Lord's Prayer* as petitions to God. I believe that, to those who are willing to engage in solitude and contemplation of the significance of each clause of *The Lord's Prayer*, some special meanings pertinent to their cultural traditions and personal concerns will become clear. Their meditation hopefully will instill ideas toward a happier and more fulfilling life.

To summarize, I would like to highlight four recurring principles mentioned in this book. Understanding and following them may help us live more calmly and peacefully.

- *as above, so below*: This principle, derived from fractals, will be explored extensively in Ch. I on OUR FATHER WHO ART IN HEAVEN.

- *more use, easier use*: This morphic field effect will be the focus of Ch. II on HALLOWED BE THY NAME.

- *persist-resist*: This tendency of attachment and its effect on us will be discussed in Ch. V on GIVE US THIS DAY OUR DAILY BREAD.

- *action-reaction*: This is generally known as *karma* and it will be examined in Ch. IV on THY WILL BE DONE ON EARTH AS IN HEAVEN and Ch. VII on LEAD US NOT INTO TEMPTATION, BUT DELIVER US FROM EVIL.

Almost all the ideas discussed herein, with the exception possibly of some models of the Creator, have been taught by various teachers or sages. I use *The Lord's Prayer* as a thread linking the precious teachings of the masters to make a rosary. I hope this book would inspire you to create your own rosary from *The Lord's Prayer*,[1] or any other prayer.

Kwan-Yuk C. SIT

New York   August 18, 2008.

---

[1]For example, Dante Alighieri (1265–1321) has an inspired version of *The Lord's Prayer* in *Purgatorio, Cantor XI* [1] and Neale D. Walsch (b. 1943) has one in *Conversations with God, Book 3* [86, p. 366].

I

Our Father Who
Art in Heaven

The Creator can be referred to as our heavenly Father or Mother depending on one's heritage or personal preference. Jesus referred to Him as *Abba*, which in Aramaic is equivalent to *Daddy*. So if we desire a more intimate relation with the Creator, we may call Him our *Daddy* or Her, our *Mommy*. The Hindus like to call Her *The Divine Mother*. The Moslems call Him *Allah*. The Taoists refer to It as *The Great Tao*.

In Buddhism, there is no mention of a Creator *per se*; its teachings state that things and events come into being only as a result of cause and effect and that Emptiness makes the laws of cause and effect possible (see *The Essence of the Heart Sutra* [30, p. 117] by The Dalai Lama (b. 1935)).

Narendra (later known as Swami Vivekananda) was the chief disciple of a Hindu holy man named Sri Ramakrishna (1836–1886). Mahendranath Gupta, another disciple and better known as M., relates in *The Gospel of Sri Ramakrishna* [46, p. 947] that

1

Narendra once discussed with Sri Ramakrishna why Buddha
Gautama (c. 563–483 B. C. E.) did not speak of God:

> He [Gautama] could not explain in words what he had
> realized by his tapasya [religious austerity]. So people
> say he was an atheist.

Sri Ramakrishna responded that Buddha was not an atheist
but Buddha simply could not explain his inner experience in
words.[1] He further added [46, p. 947]:

> Do you know what "Buddha" means? It is to become one
> with Bodha, Pure Intelligence, by meditating on That
> which is of the nature of Pure Intelligence; it is to become
> Pure Intelligence Itself.

So Buddha means the enlightened one who is simply one with
Intelligence. There is Pure Intelligence; it does not matter by
what name we call It.

Each of the terms such as Intelligence, Consciousness, Spirit,
Energy, Force, Life, and many others have been used to represent
God or an aspect of God without any particular connotation.
That is just our common usage. Heaven is not a place but
an aspect of Intelligence. It is Consciousness in a *state of
eternal bliss and infinite compassion.* The whole universe is a
manifestation of Intelligence. The Word in the Bible — used as
a figure of speech — is a reference to this manifestation aspect
of Intelligence. So is the primordial sound *aum* (also spelled as
om) in Hindu culture. It has been there from the beginning.

People with progressive leanings regard the Creator as the
Field of Infinity. Our existence and the material world are

---

[1] The Dalai Lama states that there are about ten to fourteen questions that the Buddha
never answered directly on the origin of the universe and the self. See The Dalai Lama,
The Universe in a Single Atom, [29, p. 77].

the manifestations of this Field localized in space-time. The metaphor of God as an infinite field without end is articulated eloquently by M. [46, pp. 825–826 and p. 839], who considers that the views of the infinite God are blocked by a very high wall and that great saints such as his guru Sri Ramakrishna serve as a hole in the wall through which we can see part of the meadow. Put another way, we may consider God as an infinite stage. It is as if the views of the infinite God are blocked by something like a scrim of a theater. Saints like Sri Ramakrishna provide the light that allows us to see the brightened part of the stage. Later we shall discuss how we can develop instruments to light up part of the stage for personal viewing.

In *The Way of Perfection* [72, p. 120], St. Teresa of Avila explains that "wherever God is, there is heaven" and that whenever God holds court (inside us), He is never alone. She stresses [72, p. 126] that:

> His attendants would not abandon [Him] . . .. They stay with Him and pray to Him on our behalf and for our welfare . . .

According to her, prayers are very powerful because when we pray to God, all the saints and angels are also praying to Him for us. She also states that God is everywhere and we do not have to seek Him anywhere else; like St. Augustine of Hippo (354–430), we will find God within.

This chapter is devoted to historical comments on the meaning of heaven, the idea that God the Creator is everywhere, and the observable and unobservable features of God.

The physical and spiritual aspects of Intelligence

The Chinese character 易 (pronounced *Yi* and transliterated as "I") denotes the concept common to all things that keep

changing without end—whatever intermediate state something
is in, it will change to a newer state, but there will never be a
final state. The Chinese classic *I-Ching* is a book about changes
(hence it is also widely known as *The Book of Changes*). It
expounds on the unchanging truth that Tao keeps changing.
Since antiquity, many have observed that Intelligence is always
changing. In *Conversations with God, Book 3* [86, p. 345], Neale
D. Walsch reiterates this fact clearly:

> The One Unchanging Truth is that God is always
> changing. ... The one thing that never changes is that
> everything is always changing.

An example of change is a change in location, or movement.
An idea closely associated with movement is the speed with
which a change in location occurs. In physics, speed is computed
by dividing the distance traveled by the time taken. In other
words speed is the measure of distance traveled per unit measure
of time. For a certain fixed distance from point A to point B,
if the time taken for an object to travel keeps diminishing, then
its corresponding speed must keep increasing. Assuming for the
moment the time it takes approaches zero, we may say the object
moves at a speed "approaching infinity," that is, no matter how
fast we imagine it may move, it is moving at a yet faster speed—
we cannot assign any finite value (no matter how big) to a speed
that is approaching infinity. If something could move from A to
B instantaneously, that is, if the time taken could be zero, then
its speed would be beyond measurement and mathematically
speaking, it would be considered to be moving at infinite speed.

Now, in the physical world, according to the Special Theory of
Relativity by Albert Einstein (1879–1955), no object with mass
can travel at a speed greater than the speed of light, which is
usually denoted by the symbol c, and is about 186,300 miles per
second. Since no object with mass can travel at a speed above c

(or infinite speed),[2] things that are traveling at such speeds must possess no mass and be of a spiritual nature. The assertion that God exists at the forever now may suggest that God moves with infinite speed and transcends time. I speculate that Intelligence manifests itself as Energy moving with *indefinite* speed. By indefinite speed, I mean the motion can assume speeds from zero to any value, including infinity. At zero speed, Intelligence would be in the state of complete stillness, the unfathomable "Formless" or "Void" state. At or below the speed c, all material possibilities are manifested.[3] We discern Intelligence as physical light when we sense it traveling at a speed at or below c and as spiritual light (or inner light, or clear light, or simply, light) when we "sense" it traveling at speeds above c. In this book, the upper case "Light" will be used when the non-material aspect of Intelligence is emphasized.

It is probable that It assumes all[4] the various speeds— above, at, and below c — *at the same time* and the physical and spiritual realms co-exist. We are both physical and spiritual. Many people who have had a *near death experience* (NDE) or an *out of body experience* (OBE) report that during the period when they were no longer confined to the body, whatever place or person appeared in their thought, they were right there at that location or with that person. So when we are solely in the spiritual realm, perhaps we can move at speeds above c, or even at infinite speed.

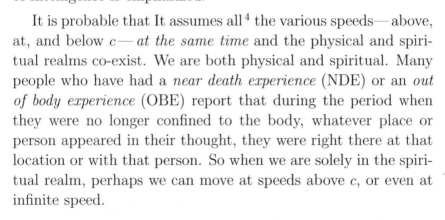

---

[2]More precisely, the limiting speed is the phase velocity c of light in a vacuum. There are superluminal experiments that can detect light pulse (or information carried by light) traveling at a group velocity in a medium faster than c. This however does not concern us or contradict Einstein. See for example Wang *et al.* [87] and also Jiang *et al.* [37].

[3]In the lecture series *GA134 The World of the Senses and the World of the Spirit*, Rudolf Steiner has an illuminating exposition of how matters arise as shattered spirit — spirit at the limit of its movement in "form." See: http://wn.rsarchive.org/Lectures/WorlSensSpir/19111230p01.html. I guess at this limiting case, spirit assumes the critical speed c.

[4]Scientists have experiments that lower the speed of light to near zero in certain media. See: http://www.hno.harvard.edu/gazette/2001/01.24/01-stoplight.html.

Please note the difference between "speed," which is defined as how *fast* an object moves from one location to another, and "frequency," which is defined as how *often* an object vibrates. For example light travels at the speed c but it vibrates as waves at different frequencies. In physics, light is considered as an electromagnetic wave, which is a fundamental component for this material world.[5] Light waves vibrating within a certain frequency range may be seen in a rainbow of colors, while those vibrating at other frequencies exhibit different characteristics and are given different names, such as infra-red or ultra-violet.

Our usual conception of light is its brightness. However, this brightness by itself cannot be perceived. It can be seen only when there is also darkness. It is the mixing of brightness and darkness, or the interaction between *yang* (brightness) and *yin* (darkness) that manifests light. Physics Professor Arthur Zajonc (b. 1949) reports in *Catching the Light* [92, p. 2] that he and a colleague once constructed a science exhibit with a certain region inside a box filled with light. When an experimenter looked through a hole into the box she saw complete darkness. Yet, if a specially placed wand outside the box was moved into this region of light, the wand appeared brilliantly lit. The experiment demonstrated that only in a world of duality can we perceive the myriad manifestations of light. In the world of entertainment, all magic light shows are clever applications of this interplay between brightness and darkness. Zajonc's exhibit indicates that in our current state of consciousness, or using our eyes as viewing instruments alone, we are incapable of perceiving the true nature of pure light. However, this does not mean the world is unreal or is a dream (though in a certain metaphorical way, it can be considered as God's dream).

---

[5] According to String Theory, the most fundamental particles of our universe are waves in the form of strings vibrating in various patterns. See for example Brian Greene (b. 1963), *The Elegant Universe* [27].

It is generally agreed that the physical sciences encompass the study of natural phenomena, including both living and non-living things. Almost all the observations in such studies are obtained either directly by our physical senses or indirectly from specially constructed instruments. Thus, they are mainly restricted to discovering those manifestations of Intelligence observable at or below the speed c. Analogously, spiritual science, or the study of spiritual phenomena, makes observations that rely on specially developed spiritual senses (which will be discussed shortly) and spiritual instruments, enabling spiritual discoveries such as the various manifestations of Intelligence perhaps detectable only at speeds above c.

We regard any school of study as a *science* if it satisfies the following two criteria.

- Any scientific theory is only a work in progress. Scientists postulate a theory about certain phenomena, subject to verification by observations. If observations support or do not contradict predictions by some proposed theory, we accept the theory as valid up to that point.

- Peers can replicate any of the reported observations by similar experiments. If a verified observation does not confirm predictions by a theory, scientists may modify that theory or replace it with a new one.

At the turn of the last century, Rudolf Steiner studied the spiritual realm using the same attitude as any physical scientist studied the physical world. He called his field of study *spiritual science* or *anthroposophy*.[6] In fact, not only Steiner but also those who pursue spiritual reality had, and have, always maintained this attitude in their research.

---

[6]Please refer to Edward R. Smith, *The Burning Bush* [60], for more information on Steiner and anthroposophy.

In *The Universe in a Single Atom* [29, p. 25], The Dalai Lama stresses this point:

> So one fundamental attitude shared by Buddhism and science is the commitment to keep searching for reality by empirical means and to be willing to discard accepted or long held positions if our search finds that the truth is different.

The Dalai Lama [29, p. 160] thinks that cognitive scientists should incorporate some training of the Buddhist meditation techniques in the study of consciousness for more substantive enrichment of physical science. Western scientists have shown great interest in establishing a physical basis for spiritual activities. They have taken bodily measurements such as heart beats, blood pressures, and brain waves of Tibetan lamas and Indian yogis in a deep meditative state. Their research has helped us understand the relation between the body and the mind or how spiritual activities have influenced the body. However, the real spiritual aspects are not captured by these physical instruments, which only measure indirectly the physical phenomena induced by the spiritual activities. This situation reminds me of a story about a boy who wants to put all the water from the ocean into a seashell but is told of its impossibility. Although the story is not a perfect analogy, we have to acknowledge that material instruments manifested by Intelligence at a finite speed below c are not adequate to investigate manifestations of Intelligence at speeds above c. We need a different kind of instrument to study the spiritual realm.

To conduct scientific research, physical scientists prepare themselves with a college education plus years of further studies in graduate schools and require an adequately equipped laboratory with institutional support. Most of their research results are beyond the general public's capability to fully comprehend. These results are frequently just reported briefly in the news and we usually accept them as exciting new knowledge.

Now let us examine how we can conduct spiritual scientific research. According to his book *How to Know Higher Worlds* [67], Steiner believed each of us has the potential to become a spiritual scientist. We are all endowed with spiritual instruments that are dormant inside our body. There are seven *chakras*[7] or "lotus flowers"[8] of energy centers within us, some of which can be developed as sense organs to perceive the spiritual world. The *chakras* are not ordinary materials or energies, but are energies moving at speeds higher than c and thus they cannot be detected by physical means. Steiner prescribed many exercises intended to nurture the development of these spiritual organs. When they become functional, Steiner called them spiritual eyes and ears. Sri Ramakrishna referred to them as "love eyes" and "love ears." He states [46, p. 115] that

> God cannot be seen with these physical eyes. In the course of spiritual discipline one gets a "love body," endowed with "love eyes," "love ears," and so on. One sees God with those "love eyes." One hears the voice of God with those "love ears."

In Buddhist traditions these organs are called celestial ears or celestial eyes. It takes many years of meditation and occult practice to develop and activate the functions of these spiritual instruments. Occasionally some people are born with spiritual instruments that are already well developed and need only to be awakened to be able to probe the spiritual realm. We may regard them as having developed instruments to light up part of

---

[7]The lower three are related to our physical body functions and the upper four, our spiritual activities.

[8]For the locations of these "lotus flowers," see for example Smith, *The Burning Bush* [60, p. 582.].

the spiritual world stage behind the scrim for their own viewing. They can see their whole body as energies and observe *chakras* as centers of these energies in the form of vortexes. Depending on their personal interests and the power of their instruments, they may report different aspects of the spiritual realm.

Steiner opines that someone with these developed instruments is not yet a *bona fide* spiritual scientist, just like one does not become an astronomer by having a telescope, or a biologist by getting a microscope. To be a spiritual scientist one still has to learn to synthesize observations from as many as twelve different viewpoints for a clear and precise comprehension of the spiritual world—the manifestation of Light at speeds above c. One special requirement for viewing spiritual phenomena is that the investigator has to be completely still and totally detached from any personal likes or dislikes. Guenther Wachsmuth (1893–1963), a dedicated student of Steiner, reports in detail in *The Life and Work of Rudolf Steiner* [83, pp. 452–453] how he first observed and studied this Light. When he sought consultation with Steiner he was surprised that he was told "not to think about this." He later understood the soundness of the advice. For if he were occupied with this thought his intellect would disturb and affect the pure viewing of the phenomena in the spiritual realm. He concludes that one must learn to be patient, "wait, observe, and wait." After an intensive training a spiritual scientist can validate observations of the spiritual world reported by others just as physical scientists do for the physical world.

According to Steiner, in the past this training was conducted orally in seclusion at *mystery centers*. [9] Nowadays, due to the progressive evolution of humankind, any aspiring student can

---

[9]In many of his lectures, Steiner described how these mystery centers in the West trained and initiated neophytes. Upon reading Taoist and Tibetan Buddhist literature, one may detect the existence of such centers in the East as well, but maybe they had not been referred to as mystery centers.

obtain the details of this training from specially written books. This does not, however, preclude private oral instructions. Steiner wrote many books and had given more than six thousand lectures on spirituality. Buddhism, Hinduism, and Taoism literatures abound with volumes about the spiritual realm.

Books of this genre (when read earnestly and with an open mind) make clear that the training for spiritual scientists is as strict and vigorous as that for the physical scientists. Shouldn't we view the validity of spiritual science with the same receptivity as we greet scientific research from the physical realm?

The Light aspect of Intelligence

Many of those who have had NDE report that after passing through a tunnel they see a very bright Light. They say that things in the spiritual realm are much more vibrant and brilliant than in our physical world. The Dalai Lama remarks that this clear light arises fully at the moment of our death.[10] Patrul Rinpoche[11] (1808–1887) describes the death process in detail and gives the exact moment when the clear light arises fully.[12]

The Dalai Lama also mentions that a very gross form of clear light will arise briefly under the following four occasions in ordinary life: yawning, sneezing, the very moment of falling asleep or fainting, and the moment of sexual climax. He further indicates that meditation can stabilize the clear light when it arises and that in certain occult practices sexual imageries are invoked by practitioners as an aid to prolong their experience of the clear light and enhance its vividness.

Dr. Elisabeth Kübler-Ross (1926–2004), an expert on death and dying, writes in her book *On Life after Death* [39, p. 45] the

---

[10]See [29, p. 157] and Hayward & Varela, *Gentle Bridges* [34, p. 81].

[11]*Rinpoche* is a title for great lamas, meaning "the precious one."

[12]See *The Words of My Perfect Teacher* [51, pp. 357–359].

following about her patients at the moment of death:

> ... very shortly before death, [they] began to relax
> deeply, to have a sense of serenity around them. And they
> were pain free, in spite of having a cancer-filled body.

That was probably the moment when the clear light arose and
returned to its Origin. The Chinese refer to this last moment of
life as the *state of the reflected Light*.

Generally, a corpse will be decomposed down to the skeleton
by bacteria and insects, despite a so-called "sealed" casket.
However, there is a report that a corpse (except for hair
and nails) totally disintegrated in seven days, and there are
also reports of unembalmed corpses that remained intact and
uncorrupted for a period varying from days to years.

The case involving the seven-day disintegration of a body is
that of a holy man reported by a well-respected Tibetan lama
Chögyam Trungpa Rinpoche (1939–1987), who was the founder
of Shambhala Training in North America. Before his death,
the holy man requested his family not to move his body for a
week. The family locked it up in a closet with a little vent for
air circulation. Occasionally family members took a peep at the
body, found it had shrunk somewhat, and observed a rainbow
outside the house. On the sixth day they found the body had
shrunk considerably. On the eighth day, when men came to
take his body to the cemetery, they did not find the body but
instead found some hair and nails on the ground. The local
lamas thought the body of the saintly man was absorbed directly
into the Light and indicated that similar occurrences had been
reported several times in the past. In *Born In Tibet* [78, p. 96],
Trungpa reported visiting the family and being shown the locked
closet as well as the remaining hair and nails. The circumstances
suggested that during that week the confined body could not
have been removed by anyone.

There are many reports of bodies remaining intact and fresh after death. We give three examples below.

As noted above, The Dalai Lama said that clear light will arise at death. He further said [34, pp. 160–161] that "some people can remain in that stage for a week, or some, twenty-two days." For example his tutor Kyabje Ling Rinpoche (1903–1983) remained for thirteen days in the state of clear light and "his body remained very fresh."

Paramhansa Yogananda (1893–1952) was an advanced Indian yogi and the founder of the Self-Realization Fellowship Organization at Los Angeles. His body was temporarily placed in a memorial park for twenty days, and according to an affidavit prepared by the Mortuary Director of the establishment, his body remained uncorrupted during that period (see Yogananda, *Autobiography of a Yogi*, [91, p. 478]).

The tomb of St. Teresa of Avila has been exhumed many times and her body showed no signs of decay (see Du Boulay, *Teresa of Avila: An Extraordinary Life* [21, pp. 266–268]). Parts of her body were even removed as holy relics.

I am not aware of any theory explaining why some bodies of saints remain uncorrupted for years or why their surroundings are permeated with pleasant fragrances. In comparison, it is widely recognized in Buddhism and Hinduism that highly accomplished meditators at the moment of death — after their last breath — can maintain a state of consciousness for a maximum of twenty-two days before finally departing their bodies. This state is referred to as *Maha-Samadhi* in Sanskrit.

In view of these accounts, we see there is more to learn about how the physical and spiritual aspects relate to one another. Each of these phenomena related to the bodies of saints, lamas, and yogis may be of a different nature. The Dalai Lama reports [29, p. 144 and p. 157] that for the sake

of scientific advancement he has convinced some lamas to let
scientists conduct experiments on them, not only during their
meditation practices as previously discussed, but also when they
are in their final clear light state, provided the scientists happen
to be present during these special moments.

The study of spiritual Light has long been a tradition of
human culture and we can find descriptions of this "Light" in a
wide range of classical texts.[13] In an essay titled **Absorption in
the Treasury of Light**,[14] Zen master Ejo (1198–1282) writes:

> *The Lotus of Truth Scripture* says, "At that time the
> Buddha radiated a Light from the white hair between
> his eyebrows, illuminating eight thousand worlds ..."

Ejo, in explaining the treasury of light, says:

> This is the Light that is not two in ordinary people and
> sages, that is one vehicle in the past and present.

In *The Life of Teresa of Jesus* [71, Ch. 38], St. Teresa of Avila
writes about her visions:

> ... while the light we see here and the other Light are
> both light, there is no comparison between the two[,] and
> the brightness of the sun seems quite dull if compared
> with the other.

Jesus said:

> If your eye is sound, your whole body will be full of light.
> — *St. Matthew*, 6:22

Probably Jesus was referring to the spiritual eyes seeing the
higher energy Light.

---

[13] In the quotes below, the word "light" is sometimes changed to "Light."

[14] See the collection *Minding Mind: A Basic Course in Meditation*, trans. by Thomas
Cleary (b. 1949) [10, p. 56–57].

In Taoism, students are taught to cultivate the *real being* from the *Golden Flower*. The Golden Flower is a symbol for the *hidden* Light.[15] When the Chinese character 金 for "gold" is partly superimposed above the character 花 for "flower," the character 光 for "Light" can be found hidden within (see Fig. 1).

金	花	金 花	金 花	光
Gold	Flower	Gold Flower	Golden Flower	Light

Figure 1. Hidden Light in Golden Flower

A practitioner who is able to stabilize this Light all the time is considered to have achieved longevity and become a real being (or immortal). The Taoist adept Lu Yen, also known as Lu Tung-pin, of the Tang Dynasty (618–907) is venerated as such a real being and *The Secrets of the Golden Flower* is a compilation of his teachings.[16]

Though the term Light is used, one does not necessarily view it as inner brightness. For instance, in *New Seeds on Contemplation* [41, pp. 219, 228, 237, 239], Thomas Merton (1915–1968) has stressed that inner darkness is "where God is hidden," and "the light of faith is darkness to the mind" but "you can rest in this darkness and this unfathomable peace." Like St. Augustine of Hippo, Merton also found God within, albeit in darkness.

---

[15]See *The Secret of the Golden Flower* [89], an English translation of the German translation from Chinese by Richard Wilhelm (1873–1930), with a commentary by Carl. G. Jung (1875–1961). Thomas Cleary, who also translated *The Secret of the Golden Flower*, but from the original Chinese version, remarked [16, pp. 276–278] that Wilhelm's German translation was based on a truncated and corrupted recension of the original work. Therefore Jung's comment on Wilhelm's translation reflected only a partial grasp of the exact meaning of the Golden Flower.

[16]See discussions on *the three meet* later for further comments on real beings and Lu Tung-pin.

The trinity aspect of Intelligence

"Three" is an important concept in all cultures.

In Christianity, the unity of Father, Son (also known as the Word), and Holy Spirit as three persons in one Godhead is known as the Holy Trinity. The Father represents the creative aspect, the Son the wisdom aspect, and the Holy Spirit the compassionate aspect.[17] The triad consisting of the Mother, the Daughter, and the Cosmic Consciousness is also used to represent the trinity aspect of God. Robert A. Powell (b. 1947) explains in his book *The Most Holy Trinosophia: The New Revelation of the Divine Feminine* [54] that this female principle has been suppressed for a long time and recently its influence has become manifest again. Andrew Harvey considers himself a messenger for the Mother. He writes in *Sun at Midnight* [33] that he had formerly projected by mistake his inspirations of the Mother onto some female guru and was fortunately awakened by the true Divine Mother.

The regular hexagram, also known as the Star of David, symbolizes the interaction between the male and the female principles.[18] An upward triangle is used to represent the three male aspects — the Father, the Son, and the Holy Spirit — while a downward triangle, the three female aspects — the Mother, the Daughter, and the Cosmic Consciousness.

In Christianity, there is no specific delineation of God as being perceivable and imperceivable, though the Father (or Mother) aspect is sometimes considered imperceivable. In Hinduism, however, there is a distinct separation. The imperceivable aspect of God is called *Brahman*. It is the Absolute and is also referred to as *Bodha*, which means Pure Intelligence

---

[17]See for example, *The Shorter Summa* [76] by St. Thomas Aquinas (1225–1274).
[18]Other interpretations are possible, such as between Form and Matter, or Man and God.

or Consciousness. It is not included in the traditional divine triad. The three perceivable aspects of God are *Brahmā* — the creative aspect, *Vishnu* — the compassionate aspect, and *Siva* — the destroying aspect. The creative aspect of God is usually referred to as the Divine Mother (also known as *Sakti*) with *Kali* being one of her many forms. Vishnu is the Preserver, similar to the Holy Spirit in Christianity. The Destroyer Siva does not have an analogue in the triune of Christianity.[19]

We summarize these terms in Table 1 below.

Aspect\Religion	Christianity	Hinduism
Imperceivable	Father/Mother	Brahman/Bodha
Creative	Father/Mother	Brahmā/Skati
Wisdom	Son/Daughter	Bodha
Compassionate	Holy Spirit/ Cosmic Consciousness	Vishnu
Destroying		Siva

Table 1. Aspects of God According to Religion

In Christianity, Jesus is regarded as an incarnation of the Son. According to Hinduism, an incarnation of God is referred to as an *avatar*. It takes an ordinary man a whole life of struggle to realize one or two aspects of God, whereas an avatar takes only a few years to realize God in all His diverse aspects. For example, Vishnu has become an avatar many times and Rāma and Krishna are two of his most revered incarnations. In the

---

[19]In Christianity, there is no special name to depict the destroying aspect of God. The Holy Spirit is said to have come after the resurrection of Jesus to endow human beings with the wisdom of compassion so that we can understand each other in spite of our differences. Brotherly love is emphasized more than the other aspects of God. In modern times, even in Hinduism there appears less reference to Siva, the destroying aspect of God.

nineteenth century, Sri Ramakrishna was tested on two separate occasions by distinguished Hindu scholars who validated his Divinity as avatar [46, p. 19]. He explains [46, pp. 98, 355, 359] that God incarnates Himself as man from time to time in order to teach people devotion and divine love. He states [46, p. 361]:

> God, incarnating Himself as man, behaves exactly like a man. That is why it is difficult to recognize an Incarnation. When God becomes man, He is exactly like man. He has the same hunger, thirst, disease, and sometimes even fear.

According to him, God plays the role of man in the world just like an actor plays a role on the stage. In *Beyond the Human Species* [82], Georges Van Vrekhem (b. 1935) relates that in the twentieth century, Sri Aurobindo (1872–1950) and his female companion Mirra Richard (1878–1973, b. Alfassa and affectionately known as the Mother) are regarded as polar incarnations of God in the male and the female.

In his book *In Search of the Miraculous* [48, pp. 77–79], P. D. Ouspensky (1878–1947) writes about *The Law of Three*, which consists of teachings of his guru G. I. Gurdjieff[20] (1872?–1949). He states that every phenomenon, on whatever scale, of whatever world, is the result of the combination or meeting of three different forces: the positive or active, the negative or passive, and the neutralizing. In the macrocosmic world the positive-negative pair can be easily seen, but the third neutralizing force cannot be observed directly. It is like the combination of the colors blue and yellow to form the color green. In G's view, green is the result of three agents interacting. The colors blue and yellow are clearly observable, but a third agent affecting how they combine is not readily discernible. The subtle action of this

---

[20]Ouspensky refers to his guru simply as G in the book.

third neutralizing force may be related to our experience that even mixing exact proportional amounts of the same blue and yellow dyes does not always produce the same shade of green. According to G, the terms active, passive, and neutralizing are only convenient names to denote the three forces. In fact each one also encompasses the three forces. It is only at their moment of meeting that each projects its dominant aspect onto the others. This property that each force encompasses all three aspects illustrates the principle that the whole is in the part. It also sheds light on the statement by Jesus to Philip:

I am in the Father and the Father in me.

— *St. John*, 14:11

In Chinese culture, the concept of "three" appears in many different areas. There are different approaches to articulate how Tao or the primordial energy of Tao manifests its three aspects. The most frequently quoted example of Tao is

- the Way of Heaven,
- the Way of Earth, and
- the Way of Man.

The Chinese philosopher Lao Tzu (c. 570–490 B. C. E.) has two comments on "three" in his classic *Tao Te Ching*. In one passage,[21] he stresses three imperceivable aspects of Tao.

Look, it can't be seen; it is called Formless.
Listen, it can't be heard; it is called Soundless.
Snatch, it can't be grasped; it is called Bodiless.
Its three attributes can't be probed
And so are mixed as one.

— *Tao Te Ching*, Ch. 14

---

[21]Most quotes of Chinese origin are my translations. For those not translated by me, the origin of the translations will be identified.

Here Lao Tzu names three attributes of Tao and yet he stresses that in general it is impossible to distinguish which is which. This implicitly coincides with the teachings of G: that each of the three forces in nature encompasses all three aspects and each only projects its dominant force when they meet.

In another passage, Lao Tzu describes three perceivable aspects:

> Tao produces one.
> One produces two.
> Two produces three.
> Three produces a myriad of things.
>
> — *Tao Te Ching*, Ch. 42

In *action*, the *one* of Tao splits into *two* equal parts. One part represents light, the active yang force. The other part represents darkness, the passive yin force. Tao keeps moving in circles, allowing the two parts to meet, at which moment a third neutralizing force is created that helps form an equilibrium. Then a myriad of things are created.

Figure 2. *Tai-ji-tu*

These passages probably inspire the *Tai-ji-tu*, the emblem of *Tai-ji* (see Fig. 2). The yang and yin forces are clearly depicted in the emblem, and the third neutralizing force is represented by an *S*-curve adjoining them. If the emblem is spinned, an infinity of shades between darkness and light will be produced until a stable state is reached. Interestingly, this emblem may also serve as an illustration of the *Law of Three* mentioned earlier by which green is described as the balanced phenomenon of the meeting of yellow (yang) and blue (yin), with a third neutralizing force mediating between them. If a model of the *Tai-ji-tu* in yellow and blue shades is spinned, then green appears.

The emblem reflects the meeting of "three" and is a symbol showing how Tao manifests. Recall that according to Lao Tzu, the three attributes of Tao are mixed as one. Thus Tao may also be simply represented by each of the two circular dots [22] in the *Tai-ji-tu*, symbolizing the idea of the whole in the part. It is an ideal example epitomizing Tao and provokes a sense of dynamic creativity.

CHIEN [1]   KUN   FU   CHIEN [2]

Figure 3. Sample hexagrams from *I-Ching*

The classic *I-Ching* (*Book of Changes*) is a treatise about how the changes of yin and yang may alter natural phenomena or the possible outcomes of our activities. It utilizes a hexagram to represent up to six possible outcomes of an event. Each outcome is presented as either a broken line (yin) or a solid line (yang). Since there are six lines, each with two possible choices there are altogether sixty-four ($64 = 2^6$) hexagrams . Fig. 3 shows four example hexagrams: CHIEN [1] has all lines solid, KUN has all lines broken, FU has all but the first line broken (counting from the bottom), and CHIEN [2] has only the third line solid. [23]

---

[22]The usual interpretation is that there is yin inside yang and yang inside yin.

[23]The transliterations for the leftmost and rightmost hexagrams in Fig. 3 are the same because their Chinese pronunciations are alike, though different. We use superscripts to distinguish them. The original Chinese can be found in the index.

In this profound classic, there is an intriguing phrase that reflects the concept of trinity and merits a closer examination. Literally the phrase in Chinese reads: "The three tardy guests come. Respect them and be auspicious in the end." [24] As we shall argue, the "three guests" is a metaphor for the three *fives* in the ancient River Diagram (Fig. 4). The eminent Taoist Liu I-Ming (1734–1821) explains the three *fives* in *Understanding Reality* [13, p. 61]:

> To the east [25] is the third element, wood; south is two [the second element], fire: fire produces wood, so fire and wood are one, together [two and three] making one five. To the west is the fourth element, metal; north is the first, water: water produces metal, so water and metal are one, together [one and four] making one five. Earth in the center constitutes one five by itself.

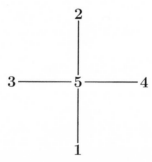

Figure 4. **Simplified River Diagram (only the first five numbers shown)**

The five elements are wood, fire, earth, metal, and water. According to Alchemical Taoism, there are two different schemes

---

[24]The Chinese original is: 有不速之客三人來，敬之終吉。 In *I-Ching*, 不速 is traditionally interpreted as "uninvited" but in other context, 不速 may mean "not fast" or "not in haste." Our translation of the phrase is similar to Cleary's [19, p. 56].

[25]Please note that the cardinal directions Liu refers to are opposite to our normal geographic orientation. For example, north is down and east is on the left.

explaining how one element produces another, depending on whether the elements are in the conditioned state or in the primordial state.

In the conditioned state, wood produces fire; fire, earth; earth, metal; metal, water; and water, wood. Each of the five elements represents not merely a natural element, but also the energy exhibiting the characteristics or functions of the natural element with the same namesake. For example, the five elements wood, fire, earth, metal, and water are considered to function respectively as regulators of our five internal organs: liver, heart, spleen, lung, and kidney. This point of view is adopted in traditional Chinese medicine practice.

In the primordial state the scheme is reversed with water producing metal; metal, earth; earth, fire; fire, wood; and wood, water [13, p. 17].

In the quoted passage on p. 22, Liu refers to the elements in their primordial state. He explains that the primordial energy has separated into the three fives, which are sometimes also called *the three yang energies* or *the three immortals.* Liu expresses and summarizes the Taoist goal (of recombining the three fives into one) in a short phrase: *"the three meet."*

According to Taoism, the three yang energies have been taken over by the human mind after our birth and become (the three) guests. It is as if they have run away and are in no haste to return. They are waiting for us to invite them back to be hosts again (for in reality we should be guests) so that they can recombine to form one primordial energy. When the three tardy guests return, we should respect them. One of the central teachings of Taoism is to nurture the three meet. Taoists regard *I-Ching* as an alchemical book on how to accomplish this (see for example, Cleary, *The Taoist I-Ching* [19]). Using the teachings of the alchemy process, they can make these three fives meet and return to their primordial state as one energy. Later in Ch. VIII

(p. 137), we shall discuss more on how yang and yin function
according to Alchemical Taoism.

The teachings of Liu echo exactly two statements from
another Taoist classic, the *Yellow Court Sutra*,[26] which may
be translated as:

> The five elements, appearing uneven, originate from the
> same root. The three fives must meet so as to return to
> one primordial essence.[27]

In Taoism, many different terms and imageries are employed
to convey the subtle idea of trinity. The purpose of fostering the
three meet is the same as realizing the Light within the Golden
Flower. Lu Yen, whom I related above as a Taoist adept and
who had realized the Light within the Golden Flower, can also
be considered as having achieved the three meet. His adopted
name Lu Tung-pin indicates this accomplishment quite plainly.
In Chinese, *Lu* is his family name, *Tung* means "cave," and *pin*
means "guest." So his adopted name signifies that "the three
tardy guests come," or have returned, to be the hosts in his
dwelling, or cave, and he is now simply a guest in this cave.
He sometimes signs his name as *Shun-yang Tze*, which means
"one with pure yang," and also implies he has purified his yang
energy within.

We have seen that different traditions have their versions of
the trinity aspect of Intelligence. If we pay attention, we may
find that the concept of three is manifested in many of our daily
experiences. Two obvious examples are time and space. For
time, there are past, present, and future; for space, there are

---

[26]The author is unknown but there is a beautiful copy of the Sutra in Chinese calligraphy.
Historically, Chinese calligraphers often copied famous Taoists or Buddhist sutras. There
is an anecdote that the famous calligrapher Wang Xizhi copied the *Yellow Court Sutra*
in exchange for several beautiful geese.
[27]In Chinese:五行參差同根節，三五合氣要本一。

front-back, left-right, and up-down.[28]   Interested readers may
consult Smith, *The Burning Bush* [60] for many examples of
threefoldness from *The Bible.*

The as above, so below aspect of Intelligence

The phrase *as above, so below* was purported to have originated
from Hermes, who used it to illustrate that the physical world
below comes from the spiritual world above. We are the physical
manifestations of the spiritual "Word."[29]   Recall that while
discussing the *Law of Three* and the *Tai-ji-tu*, I have already
touched on the idea that the part encompasses the whole. Here
I use the phrase to mean both "as spiritual, so physical" in
the sense of Hermes, and "as the whole, so the part." Let me
explore the *as above, so below* principle in the more modern and
general framework under the self-similarity or *fractal* nature of
Intelligence with several examples.   Please bear in mind that
the converse *as below, so above* is valid as well. I will illustrate
mainly the original phrase and less often its converse.

If we regard *as above* the structure of our solar system with
the sun in the center and the planets revolving around the sun,
then we may consider *as below* the structure of the atom with
the nucleus in the middle and the electrons moving around the
nucleus. In gardening we may grow a new plant from a seed, a
stem cutting, or a leaf cutting. So it is natural to view a whole
plant *as above* and such a piece of the plant *as below.*

According to acupuncture theory, pressure points that relate
to the whole body exist in many parts of the body, such as the
ear lobes, the palms of the hands, or the soles of the feet. For
example each pressure point on an ear lobe is related to an organ

---

[28]According to superstring theories, there are other hidden dimensions. See *The Elegant Universe* [27] by Brian Greene (b. 1963) and www.superstringtheory.com.

[29]See Smith, *David's Question: "What is Man?"* [61] for a detailed exposition.

of the body. Stimulating a pressure point may affect the organ corresponding to it. Thus we may take an ear lobe as *below* and our whole body as *above*.

Using a different angle, Steiner considers [60, p. 669] that our system of internal organs, as *below*, is a reflection of a portion of the solar system, as *above*. If we accept the Big Bang Theory, we may regard as *above* the material universe, which has evolved from subatomic particles after the moment of creation (the Big Bang), and as *below* a living being, which is developed from a fertilized egg after the moment of conception (a tiny bang?).

Let us look at two examples related to *as above, so below* in the sense of as physical, so spiritual. If birth from a mother's womb to the physical world through the birth canal is considered as *below*, then death from the "womb" of Mother Earth to the spiritual world through the dark tunnel[30] may be looked upon as *above*. If we treat as *above* the universe, viewing from the earth to the Milky Way, further to the outer galaxies, and still further to "Infinity," then we may regard as *below* the whole human being, going from the mind to the subconscious, deeper into our soul, and still deeper to "Emptiness."

Recently, in *Blink: The Power of Thinking without Thinking*, Malcolm Gladwell (b. 1963) discusses the concept of "thin-slicing," which is the ability of our unconscious mind to find patterns in human situations and behaviors based on very narrow slices of experience. This "thin-slicing" ability is indeed an example of the adaptive use of the *as below, so above* principle.

Henry David Thoreau (1817–1862) makes some insightful *as below, so above* observations around Walden Pond in his book

---

[30] According to studies of NDE in *The Wheel of Life* [38, p. 191] by Dr. Kübler-Ross, this transition does not have to be through a tunnel; depending on the cultural background of the person it can be through a gate, a mountain pass, a bridge, or a stream.

Walden [77, p. 275]. He comments on the comparable daily and yearly temperature changes and their consequential effects on the pond:

> The phenomena of the year take place every day in a pond on a small scale. ... The day is the epitome of the year. The night is the winter, the morning and evening are the spring and fall, and the noon is the summer.

He reports that by meticulous measurements of the pond in winter, he found out the point of greatest depth of Walden to be exactly at the intersection of the line of greatest length and the line of greatest breadth, notwithstanding the irregular shape of the pond. He surmises that this characteristic might be true for oceans, and mountains as well — for example, he notes that the highest point of a hill is not at its narrowest part. Because of his proximity with nature, probably he is justified to assert [77, p. 265] the following:

> If we knew all the laws of Nature, we should need only one fact, or the description of one actual phenomenon, to infer all the particular results at that point.

It seems that Thoreau is very adept at "thin-slicing." What is interesting is his observation of the connection between the pond and ethics [77, p. 265]:

> ... draw lines through the length and breadth of the aggregate of a man's particular daily behaviors and waves of life into his coves and inlets, where they intersect will be the height or the depth of his character.

Although he does not use the phrase *as below, so above*, he is clearly well versed in the relation between the whole and the part and between the physical and the spiritual.

Some models of Intelligence

Depending on which aspect of Intelligence we want to emphasize, we may consider different models. We begin with two simple ones and then proceed to more elaborate models.

An Onion Model

Sri Ramakrishna used an onion as a metaphor [46, p. 148] to illustrate the "Emptiness" nature of God. After peeling off a layer from an onion, we still have the shape of the onion. When the last layer of the onion is peeled away, "nothing" is left.

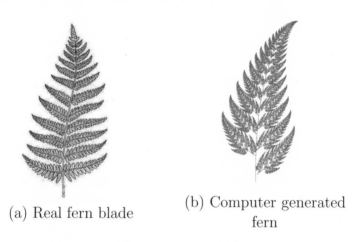

(a) Real fern blade

(b) Computer generated fern

Figure 5. Fern Leaves

A Fern Leaf Model

Many objects in nature illustrates the *as above, so below* principle esthetically. A fern leaf is an example showing this beautiful fractal nature — any smaller branch of the fern leaf when enlarged looks exactly like a whole fern leaf. So the part does have the whole within. Fig. 5 shows that a computer program can make use of this property to simulate the picture of a real fern blade.

The Sierpinski's Triangle Model

Sierpinski's triangle is an excellent model to illustrate several subtle aspects of Intelligence, and is particularly relevant to the trinity aspect. The fractal nature of the triangle may be visualized in many ways and the one illustrated in Fig. 6 is generated by a randomized method called Chaos Game. Points are scattered inside the generated figure in a special pattern. At a glance we see that the triangle is subdivided into four smaller triangles, where the one in the center is blank and the three surrounding triangles are "littered with" points. Looking more closely we see that each of the surrounding smaller triangles has the same pattern as the original big triangle. In particular there is always a central triangular portion that is blank and this blank center is present in every non-blank small triangle. Thus it shows the *as above, so below* principle like a fern leaf does. We now briefly describe the Chaos Game algorithm.[31]

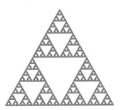

Figure 6. Sierpinski's Triangle

Start with a blank triangle *ABC*. Pick a point *X* as a reference point inside the triangle (see Fig. 7(a) on p. 30). Mark the point *X* with a dot. Randomly pick a vertex, say *B*. Mark with a dot the point *Y* which is mid-way between *X* and *B* along

---

[31]You may see how Sierpinski's triangle emerges and learn in detail how to play the Chaos Game by visiting http://www.jcu.edu/math/vignettes/ChaosGame.htm. You may also simply view the emergence of Sierpinski's triangle at http://www.cut-the-knot.org/Curriculum/Geometry/SierpinskiChaosGame.shtml.

the line $\overline{XB}$ (see Fig. 7(b)). [32] The above procedure is repeated with Y taking the role of X as the new reference. After enough repetitions, the pattern of Sierpinski's triangle will emerge. [33]

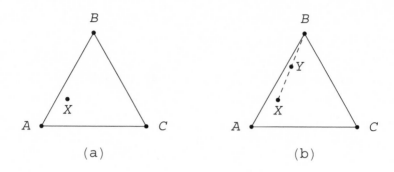

Figure 7. Start of Chaos Game

With this model, we consider the three vertices as the three attributes or forces of Intelligence and the space inside the triangle as the sphere of activity of the three forces. The algorithm is a description of how the three forces interact. Each position where a dot appears may be regarded as where the three forces meet. The dots represent a myriad of perceivable manifestations of Compassion, illustrating Lao Tzu's "three produces a myriad of things." The empty space within the triangle is viewed as the unfathomable void, which is nonetheless saturated with eternal bliss and pregnant with all possibilities.

This Void aspect of Intelligence is called *Christ Consciousness* or *Godhead* in Christianity, *Brahman* in Hinduism, *Thusness* or *Buddha nature* in Buddhism, and *the Mystic Female* or *the Mysterious Pass* in Taoism.

---

[32] The line $\overline{XB}$ in Fig. 7(b) is for illustration only and should not be drawn.

[33] If it happens that the initial point of reference is inside the central smaller triangle, then all the points obtained afterward will be outside (in fact a mathematician can prove this). Afterward, simply disregard this initial point.

This model illustrates that we are all One with the same characteristics. Using this model we can easily comprehend the metaphorical meaning of statements made by Zen masters and Taoists. For example, from the translations by Thomas Cleary, we find in *The Secret of the Golden Flower* [16, 3.15, p. 286]:

The center is omnipresent;
the whole universe is within it.

and in *The Flower Ornament Scripture* [8, p. 339]:

What in one atom is manifest
Is also manifest in all atoms.

If we treat the whole Sierpinski's triangle as God, and small triangles inside as objects such as human beings, animals, trees, or stones, then the idea that every object is also God or has God's nature would be easy to grasp and no longer mysterious. In fact not only material objects demonstrate this fractal feature, any repeating activity subject to some set of rules will have this fractal characteristic. This fractal nature of Intelligence is exactly what Krishna, an avatar of Vishnu, told his disciple Arjuna, as related in *The Bhagavad Gita* [24, 5.18] :

They see the same Self in a spiritual aspirant and an outcast, in an elephant, a cow, and a dog.

and in [24, 6.29]:

... the Self in every creature and all creation in the Self.

Sri Ramakrishna reportedly mentioned in one of his visions [46, p. 21] that:

... he saw the Ultimate Cause of the universe as a huge luminous triangle giving birth every moment to an infinite number of worlds.

His vision of the triangle does confirm the appropriateness of using Sierpinski's triangle as a model of Intelligence, which fittingly illustrates the idea that we are all alike and have Godhead inside us.

As a last example, this idea is also expounded by 9th Century Zen master Changsha[34] (italics added):

> The whole universe is the eye of a practitioner.
> The whole universe is the family talk of a practitioner.
> The whole universe is the total body of the practitioner.
> The whole universe is one's own light.
> *In the whole universe there is no one who is not oneself.*

An Elastic Line Model

We now consider an open interval, which is a line segment excluding its two end points, as our next model of Intelligence. In mathematics, an infinite straight line is also considered as an open interval.

An open interval enjoys a special property: For *every* point inside an open interval, we can construct a small open interval centered around it that lies completely inside the original open interval. This is because every point of an open interval must be at a non-zero distance from either end of the line segment.[35] The infinite line also has this special property.

We can imagine the open interval being so elastic that it can be stretched and extended or shrunk and diminished to any length. Together with the special property, this elasticity,

---

[34]See Ejo, Absorption in the Treasury of Light, in the collection *Minding Mind*, translated by Cleary [10, p. 62].
[35]We emphasize that this property must be true for *every* point. If the line segment includes any of the two end points, then no matter how small an open interval is centered at that end point, half of this small interval always lies outside the original line segment.

which can be precisely expressed mathematically,[36] enables us to regard any small open interval centered at any point as similar to the original open interval. Thus, open intervals have the self-similarity or fractal property.

Generally, we may regard the universe as a manifestation of Intelligence and the center of the universe may be anywhere. If an open interval is considered as the whole universe and its midpoint as the center, then by the fractal property above, every point in the open interval will also be the center of the universe. The model clearly reflects the *as above, so below* aspect of Intelligence. Furthermore, when an open interval is stretched continuously it will approach the infinite line and when it is shrunk indefinitely it will become infinitesimally small and approach the empty set.[37] Thus the open interval also mirrors both the infinity and emptiness aspects of Intelligence. This aptly illustrates the description about the opening of the Mysterious Pass in Taoism (Cleary, *Practical Taoism*, [15, p. 519]):

So vast there is no outside,
Yet so minute there is no inside.

Circle Models

A circle has several very rich symbolic meanings that can be used to illustrate the Trinity and Oneness aspects of Intelligence.

To use a circle to illustrate the Trinity aspect, we consider (see Fig. 8(a), p. 34) its center as the Father, the point moving in the circumference as the Son, and the radius as the Holy Spirit,

---

[36]Stated simply, there is a homeomorphism (or continuous bijection) between a finite open interval and the infinite line, and hence there is also one between any two finite open intervals.

[37]In contrast, a line segment including both endpoints is not homeomorphic to the infinite line, and when shrunk indefinitely, will result in a single point when the two end points meet.

which keeps the point moving in the circle without veering off
tangentially or collapsing into the center.

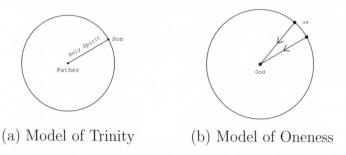

(a) Model of Trinity   (b) Model of Oneness

Figure 8. Circle Models of Trinity and Oneness

A circle is also a good model to illustrate the Oneness of
our existence. Consider two distinct points on the circle (see
Fig. 8(b)). No matter how close they are, we can always locate
points between them. In other words, they are two separated
entities. However, if the two points move inward along the two
radii, they would come to the same center. Metaphorically God
is our center projecting Himself onto the space-time universe.
Therefore as projection points we are distinct, but going within
we all have the same Godhead or Origin. We shall revisit these
ideas in Ch. VII, p. 117 and p. 127.

By examining the geometric relations between a circle and a
straight line, we can also use a circle to model the cyclic aspect
of Intelligence, which will now be explored.

A circle is often used to represent the cyclic attribute of Tao
since Tao keeps changing and always returns to where it starts.
Lao Tzu stresses repeatedly this cyclic aspect of Tao (italics
added):

Continually threading on, it [Tao] is indefinable and
returns beyond the realm of things.

— *Tao Te Ching*, Ch. 14

All things flourish yet each one *returns* to its root.

— *Tao Te Ching*, Ch. 16

As great as if it [Tao] disappears
It disappears to a far away place;
From a far away place it *returns*.

— *Tao Te Ching*, Ch. 25

We are going to illustrate how a straight line and a circle together can deepen our understanding of the concept "return" as used by Lao Tzu.

We can perceive a circle being formed when a straight line is bent so that the extremities at infinity extending to each of the two directions of the line are merged as one (which turns up as a point on the circle). Or we can imagine removing a point from the circle and flattening the arc to become a line segment without its end points, which is thus a finite open interval. Nevertheless, using the elastic line model we can regard it as a straight line extending at both ends indefinitely.

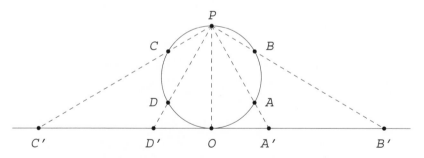

Figure 9. Relation of Circle to Infinite Line

Let me describe briefly (without going into details with justification) how to associate each point on a circle with a point on a straight line and *vice versa*. Assume we have a horizontal line and a circle touching at O as shown in Fig. 9. Draw the vertical diameter OP. The point O, which lies on both the circle and the line, is regarded as corresponding to itself. The point P will correspond to no points on the straight line and may be considered as corresponding to the two identified extremities of the straight line at infinity. We now draw from P a slant line segment meeting the circle and the horizontal line. The two intersecting points will form a corresponding pair. So for example we have A corresponds to A', B to B' and so on.

To grasp Lao Tzu's idea of return, let us imagine a tiny worm crawling around a big circle. Suppose it starts at point O and moves on, passing points A, B, P, C, D, and back to O again (see Fig. 9, p. 35). Because of the worm's smallness in size compared to the big circle, it would have the illusion that it is always going along some straight road rather than a curve. The tiny worm probably considers that it is going along the same straight line: from O to A', B' and so on. When the worm passes point P on the circle it may think that it has gone so far even to infinity "beyond the realm of things." As it continues to points C, D and back to O on the circle, it might have the impression that it is returning to O from C', D' on the other side of the straight line. To this tiny worm, its journey is really amazing, for somehow "it disappears to a far away place;" yet "from a far away place it returns." The cyclic attribute of Tao can be articulated elegantly and succinctly by means of this straight line idiom. Each of our activities is like a worm starting from us and brings its effect back to us. The maxim "as ye sow, so shall ye reap" (*Galatians*, 6:7) is simply an alternative way of saying this return or cyclic principle of our activities.

There are numerous analogies of this cyclic phenomenon in nature and in life that are related by the *as above, so below* principle. As an illustration, we consider the cyclic phenomena of breathing and sleeping. We continuously inhale and exhale each day and repeatedly alternate between a waking and sleeping state of consciousness through our life. If we regard the total number of our breaths in a day as *below*, then we may view the total number of days in our life-span as *above*. Supposing on the average we take 18 breaths in a minute. In an hour we will have taken 1,080 breaths and in a day 25,920 breaths.[38] *As above, so below*, the average life span of a person will be about 25,920 days or about 71 years.[39] When 71 is rounded to the nearest tens, it will be exactly as mentioned in the Bible: "the years of our life are three scores and ten" (*Psalms*, 90:10).

This statement in the Bible is more relevant to people in ancient times. In the past, people lived more closely with the rhythm of nature. Modern people lead a life style quite independent of nature's cycle of day and night. For example, they now seldom get up at sunrise or rest after sunset. Even though people still live twenty-four hour days, some workers are required to stay awake for consecutive days or need to be awakened from sleep for emergency work. So we should no longer use this statement as an indicator for our life expectancy.

The number 25,920 is also related to the great circle of the sun, a cyclic phenomenon in nature. The vernal point of the zodiac, where the sun rises at spring equinox, keeps advancing. It advances from one constellation to the next every 2,160 years. There are twelve constellations and it takes 25,920 years for the sun to make one complete great circle. So as *below*, we take 25,920 breaths in a day and as *above*, the sun takes 25,920 years to make one complete round through the zodiac.

As a final example, suppose we regard as *above* the rotations of the earth around its axis day after day and the changes

---

[38]The total number of breaths in a day is computed as follows: Since one hour equals 60 minutes, we have $18 \times 60 = 1,080$ breaths in an hour, and since one day equals 24 hours, we have $1,080 \times 24 = 25,920$ breaths in one day.

[39]We are interested only in whole number of years. Dividing 25,920 by 365 we get approximately 71.

through the four seasons of spring, summer, autumn and winter year after year, then we may regard as *below* the alternation of our consciousness between sleeping and waking day after day and the progress from the four stages of birth, aging, illness, and death life after life. From this perspective, reincarnation[40] is just one attribute of our existence like other cycles in nature. The cyclic phenomena of nature and *as above, so below* principle have helped us grasp the concept of reincarnation.

The Möbius Band Model

This model may be used to illumine the "no inside or outside" aspect of Intelligence, which we will explore after a brief discussion of the model.

Take a strip of paper and glue the opposing ends of the strip together. An open short cylinder will be formed: one surface of the paper becomes the inside surface of the cylinder and the other becomes the outside. The two surfaces of the cylinder are separated by the circular rims. When we trace a line around the cylinder (starting from either outside or inside) we can never get to the other surface without going over one of the rims.

Now take another strip of paper, twist the strip half a turn — one hundred eighty degrees — and glue the opposing ends of the strip. The resulting strip[41] is no longer the cylinder above and is called a *Möbius band*. One surface of the "cylinder" (or paper) has been joined to the other surface and the two "rims" become one edge due to the twist. We can mark a pencil trace along the length of the band continuously without going over the edge

---

[40] According to anthroposophy, reincarnation is not just an Eastern concept. Indeed, it was accepted by the West up to the time of Jesus. However, it was not to be taught in the West for two thousand years in order that Christianity might develop. See for example, *The Soul's Long Journey* by Edward R. Smith [62].

[41] If we imagine the strip to be very narrow, then the shape looks like the mathematical symbol ∞ for infinity.

and return to the starting point, and in one complete round, the trace has traversed both surfaces of the paper. The Möbius band has only one surface (and one edge), and hence on that surface, there is no orientation of inside or outside.

This real object helps us understand similar abstract references in Taoists and Buddhists teachings. When they say "going within" or "look inward" they do not really mean inspecting under our skin and studying our internal organs as in medical practice. The teaching of looking inward [16, 4.24, p. 290] emphasizes this aspect of no inside or outside:

> Not looking outward yet being alert is inward looking; it is not that there really is such a thing as looking inward.

This is also a noted aspect of Buddhahood (see Cleary, *Buddhist Yoga: A Comprehensive Course*, [9, p. 2], italics added):

> He [the Buddha] realized the boundless equanimity of Buddhahood, with *no inside or out*, corresponding [to] the cosmos, throughout all space and time.

Alternatively we may hold the polar perspective that God is both within and without us. That was how St. Teresa of Avila felt [71, p. 119]:

> I used unexpectedly to experience a consciousness of God, of such a kind that I could not doubt that He was within me or that I was wholly engulfed in Him.

The Mandelbrot Set and Julia Sets Model

Another astounding and elegant model is that of *Mandelbrot set* and *Julia sets* (MJS) from Chaos Theory. Readers probably have already seen the beautiful graphics of the MJS. Let us study the relation between the Mandelbrot set and Julia sets[42] as shown in Fig. 10. Here, the dark central figure is the Mandelbrot set. To each point of the Mandelbrot set there corresponds a Julia set. The insets show the Julia sets associated with different points near the Mandelbrot coastline. By inspecting and comparing the Julia sets in Part (a) and Part (b) of Fig. 10, we can observe how the Julia sets corresponding to relatively close locations along the Mandelbrot coastline share somewhat similar patterns.

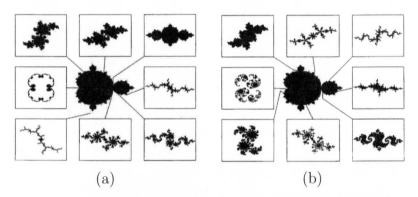

(a)   (b)

Figure 10.   (a) Mandelbrot set for $z^2 - \lambda$, decorated with varous Julia sets and filled Julia sets. (b) Same as (a). These often resemble the place on the boundary from which they come, especially if one magnifies up enough. Reproduced by permission from Michael Barnsley, *Fractals Everywhere* [2, Fig. 8.3.2].

If we regard the surface of our planet as the coastline of the Mandelbrot set and our human attributes such as cultural traditions, facial features and body frames as Julia sets, then at different regions of the earth there are different cultural traditions, facial features and body frames reflecting its locality. Furthermore, nearby countries exhibit variations of similar traits of those human attributes. The fractal features of the

---

[42]For an interactive illustration of fractal features of the MJS, visit the website created by Robert Devaney: http://www.ibiblio.org/e-notes/MSet/Anim/ManJuOrb.htm.

MJS model illustrate that location plays a subtle role in our civilization and our evolution.

The graphics of the MJS shown here are obtained using a particular family of similar functions[43] and they reflect how the values (or points) are affected by these functions after repeated evaluations. Such repeated evaluations are called *iterations.*[44] It turns out that certain intrinsic properties about these iterations are demonstrated by the MJS. For different families of similar functions the associated MJS may look very different from that shown in Fig. 10 (p. 40), yet these intrinsic characteristics remain unchanged (see Appendix).

Figure 11. A zoom on a piece of the boundary of the Mandelbrot set for $z^2 - \lambda$**.**   Reproduced by permission from Michael Barnsley, *Fractals Everywhere* [2, Fig. 8.3.3].

From these graphics we see that the Mandelbrot set may be regarded as a map whose surroundings reveal the characteristics of its associated Julia sets. A piece of the coastline of the Mandelbrot set (Fig. 11) and a Julia set corresponding to a

---

[43]Please refer to the Appendix if you are interested in the formulae of the functions and some basic terms in Chaos Theory.

[44]In nature and our daily life, iteration constantly occurs. An obvious example is the growth of cells.

typical location (Fig. 12) are zoomed to show their details. Note how the piece of the coastline of the Mandelbrot set always reveals a familial resemblance of its associated Julia sets. We have used this intrinsic characterization as a model to illustrate our cultures and evolutions. We are going to see that this intrinsic relationship is also a good model for physiognomy and for *Feng-shui*.

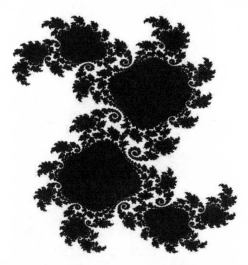

Figure 12. A filled Julia set corresponding to the piece of the coastline of the Mandelbrot set in Fig. 11. Note the family resemblances. Reproduced by permission from Michael Barnsley, *Fractals Everywhere* [2, Fig. 8.3.4].

Our facial features encompass a wealth of information about us, allowing specially trained oriental physiognomists to read and interpret our destinies accurately.[45] Each being may be viewed as the coastline of the Mandelbrot set of the functions of its soul. Its belongings and body features correspond to Julia

---

[45]There is an interesting discussion about how scientists have learned that the face actually manifests a person's inner emotions openly. See Malcolm Gladwell, *Blink: The Power of Thinking without Thinking* [26, pp. 206–208].

sets. The objects or features would retain certain aspects of the being that are seldom noticed. But people with well honed ESP abilities can feel an object and describe various traits of its owner. Inspecting the associated Julia set — the object — can reveal certain characteristics of the coastline of the Mandelbrot set — its owner. The saying that "all belongings reflect their owner" merely expresses this MJS relationship.

Feng-shui is the study of the relation between the habitat and its inhabitants. According to *Feng-shui* theory, a place has significant influence on its inhabitants. The practitioners can explain how the landscape of a place reflects the interactions among the five elements,[46] the overall force of which will indicate whether the area is beneficial, bringing great prosperities, or harmful, bringing disasters or distress.[47] They apply their observations from nature and advise their clients to create beneficial living arrangements in their homes so as to enhance and foster their well-being.[48] The general consensus in the practice of *Feng-shui* is that the overall environment affects the welfare of the society as a whole whereas the local venue is more relevant to an individual. Therefore, even he who lives in a supposedly adverse area can still bring relatively good fortune to himself if he can create a local setting that promotes a good influence.

If we consider that Tao or Intelligence manifests its energies via the five elements, then the constant manifestation of the

---

[46]The five elements are wood, fire, earth, metal, and water. In this order wood produces fire but opposes what fire produces, namely earth. Continuing this scheme we will have water produces wood but opposes what wood produces, namely fire. See also the reference to the five elements in our discussion of the three meet.

[47]There are also *Feng-shui* theories indicating which of the five elements are more significant during different periods of time. However, the topic is beyond the scope of this brief exposition.

[48]Here only very crude effects of *Feng-shui* are discussed. In Chinese culture, the livelihood of an individual depends on destiny first, fortune second, *Feng-shui* third, past good deeds fourth, and study and learning fifth. Personal endeavors are also important factors. *Feng-shui* is not the most important factor in affecting the success and well-being of an individual.

various combinations of these energies through time can be
considered as iterations of a family of similar functions of Tao.
The coastlines of the Mandelbrot set are the environments and
the Julia sets are the objects as well as the consequences, such
as cultures, body features, and in particular the consequences
of prosperities and misfortunes, as emphasized in *Feng-shui*.
From this perspective we can see why we have the environment
reflecting our cultural traditions as observed earlier and why in
general *Feng-shui* works.

Conclusion

We should remember that we have choosen different models to
high-light different aspects of Intelligence and we should not
fixate on the aspects represented by one model and forget the
other aspects. For example, while Origin is viewed as the center
in a circle model, it is considered to be everywhere in the elastic
line model as well as in the model using Sierpinski's triangle.
Still, readers should recall that according to Lao Tzu, the Origin
cannot be seen, heard or grasped.

Studies on NDE inform us that those who have had NDE
would not talk much about their experience to others. Even if
they would write books years later to report what happened to
them, their report would probably convey a very small portion
of their overall experience. It is not that these people intend
to keep things to themselves; but rather, the whole experience
is just beyond words. Therefore any description is only a very
fragmented and incomplete personal expression.

Sri Ramakrishna explains [46, pp. 102–103, 358] that those
who have experienced Cosmic Consciousness or seen God are
unable to talk about the experience because it would be like a
doll made of salt trying to measure the depth of the ocean: it
would be dissolved in the ocean and unable to make a report.

What has been presented is an introductory and preliminary exploration to understand some aspects of Intelligence. If we delve more deeply into Buddhism or any esoteric studies of the Absolute, we would encounter the repeated assertion that the Absolute cannot be described.

Our perception of Intelligence is not much different from a frog's vista of the sky at the bottom of a well. It is not that the sky is small, only the frog's view is limited! Lao Tzu says:

> Those who know, won't say.
> Those who say, don't know.
>
> — *Tao Te Ching*, Ch. 56

These statements can be understood to mean that those who know that their knowledge is incomplete won't say, while those who say do not know that their knowledge is incomplete. So please excuse my indulgence in presenting this incomplete study, violating the dictum of Lao Tzu.

II

Hallowed Be
Thy Name

We know Godliness implies holiness, which we can neither enhance nor deplete. By inference, the name of God is holy (that is, hallowed). When Moses experienced the presence of God in the burning bush and wanted to know His name, he was answered: [1]

"I Am Who I Am."

— Exodus 3.14.

This indicates that there is no need to call God by any particular name. In Ch. I (p. 31) we illustrated that each of us has God within. Each of us refers to this inner Self as "I Am." God wanted Moses (and us) to call Him "I Am" because He is our inner Self.

---

[1]See also *The Burning Bush* [60, pp. 244–282] by Edward R. Smith for a detailed exploration of the meaning of "I Am."

We are not in this world to bring additional holiness to the *name* of God. We are here to live and bring out the "holiness" of our inner Self. Most of us care about our family names and regard following our family steps as a respectful way to honor our parents. Only when we remember who we are and what we are here for will we then not repeat the misery of the prodigal son. *As above, so below*, the way to honor the name of Our Father would be to continue His work on earth. Since Our Father is the Creator, our work will be re-creation. Jesus makes this very clear:

> Let your light so shine before men, that they may see your good works and give glory to your Father who is in heaven.
>
> — *St. Matthew*, 5:16

The idea of re-creation has been thoroughly elucidated in the trilogy *Conversations with God* by Neale D. Walsch [84,85,86]. According to Walsch [86, p. 357], we are not here to suffer or to learn any lessons, but to participate in re-creation so as "to experience the next grandest version of the greatest vision" we've ever had of Who We Are![2] Indeed Jesus re-created the grandest version of Himself. He shed light on the true meaning of HALLOWED BE THY NAME.

Since God created everything "long ago," we are *not* here to create, but to re-create. I discussed in Ch. I (p. 5) that in the Absolute, there is no time. God is always in the forever now. So "long ago" is only a term for our convenience to refer to a certain event or aspect of Intelligence. We may imagine that God "has created" or still "is creating" an infinite number of worlds and we are re-creating along one particular world line. Using Sierpinski's triangle model we may regard ourselves as

---

[2]Walsch used the phrase "I've ever had of Who I Am!"

the smaller triangles manifesting together with the Godhead. In other words, we are *co*-creating with God. Depending on our perspective we may consider that we are either re-creating, or co-creating, with God. We are confined in space–time but our Creator transcends space–time. It is inconceivable to us that we can be at different locations doing different things at the same time. But to Infinity, being everywhere at the same time is one of Its natural states of consciousness. An approximate imagery to this omnipresence of Intelligence is the picture of the pyramid on the back of the U. S. one-dollar bill. We are confined in space–time at the bottom of the pyramid, whereas God is the ever-seeing eye at the top, transcending space–time.

According to anthroposophy or spiritual science, Yahweh created all the forms or archetypes in the ether — a form of energy vibrating at a speed above *c*. Alternatively, according to Walsch [86, p. 117] in the words of God:

> The Eternal Moment contains all "possible possibilities."
> ... All that's left is for you to make some perception choices.

Any concept or any material manifestation on the earth plane is a resonance with, or a re-creation of, one of the created forms or possibilities in the ether. If such a form or possibility has never been manifested on this earth, it may take a great deal of effort to make it appear. But once a resonance has been made, the form or possibility will be manifested with continuously less effort by its repeated appearances.

In *A New Science of Life* [58, pp. 49–52] and *The Presence of the Past* [59, pp. 97–114], Rupert Sheldrake (b. 1942) theorizes that an activity, either physical or mental, is like a ball rolling down a field. In the first few attempts the ball may not roll smoothly or precisely on the desired course, but with repetitions the ball will roll easier. In other words: *more use, easier use,* a principle which Sheldrake illustrates with various examples, such as chemicals forming new crystals [58, pp. 103–107] and animals learning new tricks [59, pp. 173–177]. He has conducted experiments to prove this *more use, easier use* principle where people solve difficult new visual puzzles [58, pp. 250–256]. He conjectures that there is a morphic field for each activity, and each repetition makes resonance with the field easier. His original exposition is quite technical. Here, the theory has been greatly simplified and the concepts restated in simple terms. In fact, even without Sheldrake's morphic field theory, we can realize the validity of the *more use, easier use* principle in the saying "practice makes perfect." We have only to watch a toddler practice walking, and see how easily he soon will walk. Sheldrake's introduction of the terms morphic field and morphic resonance[3] provides us with language to more efficiently discuss this *more use, easier use* phenomenon.

Experience shows that *easier use, more use,* the converse of *more use, easier use,* is also true. Let me give a plausible reason for this converse phenomenon. The performance of an activity possibly would generate a "spiritual magnetic force" in its morphic field, just as a traveling electron in an electric circuit would generate a magnetic force in the electric field. Similar to the phenomenon in physics that there are different ways to generate magnetic fields, there would be different ways to generate spiritual magnetic fields. Each type of activity would have its own field. Repeating an activity would be like increasing its spiritual current. A stronger spiritual current would generate a bigger spiritual magnetic force and attract more inclinations to this activity, just like a bigger magnet would attract more iron filings. In other words, *easier use* will engender *more use.*

---

[3]Please visit his website at http://www.sheldrake.org/intro/ to explore more.

Indeed the idea of spiritual magnetic force would be a reasonable way to explain the phenomenon of trends or fads. An activity that is in vogue acts like a huge magnet and will attract many followers, thus becoming an even bigger and stronger magnet. But there are also people not affected by a fad. Probably they have very strong will power or are absorbed in some other kind of activities. Thus they have no resonance with this fad at this moment. It is their intent that determines whether they will be attracted to a fad or not. As time progresses, a fad probably dies down because other kinds of fads or trends are created, drawing people's attention to them instead. The effects of the earlier fads are still present and can be rekindled at any time when enough people carry out the activities again.

When we are attracted to an activity, we are captured by its morphic field and that is the reason we find it difficult to change our habits. We need to devise a new activity with a different morphic resonance to interfere with or dampen the effect of the spiritual magnetic force of the original activity. Sometimes a special ritual may be enough. But in general, it will take a strenuous effort and a committed determination to recondition our habitual activities. Maybe that is why in *St. Matthew*, 5:29–30, we are given the drastic advice to pluck out the eye or cut away the hand that sins in order to avoid being thrown into hell. We really have to be careful when we decide to carry out a particular activity; for if it becomes habitual it will be very hard to change. If we have weak will power and do not want to get addicted to some undesirable activity, not only should we avoid those who are practicing it, we should even avoid entertaining the thought of performing it. We do not want to generate a resonance to its field and get attracted by its force.

Thoughts, like *actions*, create morphic resonances. Their morphic effect on the individual may not be as strong as actions.

If a thought, like an activity, is repeated frequently enough, the morphic effect may strengthen sufficiently to become as powerful as that from an action. For example, in his book *Our Endangered Values: America's Moral Crisis* [6, pp. 65–66], former President Jimmy Carter (b. 1924) recounts that in his *Playboy* interview in November 1976, he quoted a passage from *The Gospels* (*St. Matthew*, 5:28) in which Jesus said that anyone "who looks at a woman lustfully has already committed adultery with her in his heart." Carter admits he "had felt sexual desire for some girls" he had known. He recalls that, while he did not commit actual adultery, there was a fire storm of criticism from his political opponents and famous church leaders because of his "lust," and within a week, he lost "10 percentage points in public opinion polls." This story illustrates how the strong morphic effect associated with thoughts and discussions about thoughts may propagate and multiply.

The *more use, easier use* principle can be applied to thoughts and their spiritual magnetic force can empower our abilities in a constructive fashion. Indeed, we can make use of the principle to change our undesired habits through deliberate will power. Every time that we are tempted to carry out a certain undesirable habitual activity we shall remind ourselves not to succumb to that attraction. In the beginning we probably will fail to stop performing that activity. But after dedicated and frequent repetitions of asserting such determination we may succeed once and then twice, just like toddlers striving to walk. We will eventually overcome that binding force of our bad habit.

The above example, albeit about a very difficult endeavor, illustrates the beneficial effect of using the mind to overcome our undesirable habits. There are many indications that undertaking mental practice may enhance a skill just as effectively as actually practicing it. This is really an application of the morphic field effect.

The great pianist Artur Rubinstein (1887–1982) reported in *My Many Years* [57, p. 198] an anecdote about how he practiced in his mind. Once he was asked to perform César Franck's *Variations Symphoniques*, a piece he had never played before, in two days' time. The performance was in a different city and he had to take a long train ride. Upon his arrival, the rehearsal would be an hour, and the concert six hours later. He only had time to read the score on the train trip. He studied the score carefully and tried difficult passages on his lap during the journey. He explained that due to the pressure of publicity he decided not to use the score even for the rehearsal and was able to play without stopping. He then used the remaining hours to actually practice with a piano to refine the details. Rubinstein was an amazing master in this kind of mental gymnastics.

Another example is mind training. There are reports[4] that some athletes induce themselves to dream lucidly — to become aware that they are dreaming — so they can hone their skills even in their dreams.

The influence of the *more use, easier use* principle is amazingly wide and deep. The calming or healing effects of prayers such as *The Lord's Prayer*, or *Hail Mary*, or mantras such as *aum* (*om*) or "*om mani padme hum*" may be easily realized by a sincere seeker because these prayers have been recited with effectiveness by many in the past.

The morphic fields of our activities can be viewed as a record of our history. It is called an *akashic record*[5] in Sanskrit or a *celestial book* in Chinese. This record is like our footprints in the snow or sand. Whereas those in the snow or sand may melt or

---

[4]See the article Applications of Lucid Dreaming in Sports by Paul Tholey (1937–1998), http://gestalttheory.net/people/thol_ref.html.

[5]According to Rudolf Steiner, in his book, *Life Between Death and Rebirth* [64], an akashic record is also created, albeit in a different manner, in the even higher astral plane after our death.

be washed away, an akashic record will be kept indefinitely for our reference. It is to be used for our future development and is presented to us as a series of panoramic images right after our death. This phenomenon of life-review has been widely reported by those who have had a near death experience. Persons with their functioning spiritual eyes and ears can read — perceive images of — the akashic records of others and world events.[6] The clarity of their perception depends on how advanced they have developed these particular abilities. The sleeping prophet Edgar Cayce (1877–1945) was one such famous person having occult or psychic ability.[7] Rudolf Steiner was perhaps another exemplifying this ability to its fullest in the modern world.[8]

The morphic field can explain why it is not infrequent that two or three different people have similar discoveries independently at roughly the same time. When the physical world is ready to manifest a new idea, anyone having a vigorous resonance with that field may bring out the manifestation. Of course, those who have been working on the concept would have a greater opportunity to resonate more coherently and become the pioneering innovators, many of whom have mentioned inspira-tions at odd moments. Some even reported specific imageries while they are dreaming. As examples, Elias Howe (1819–1867), the inventor of the first patented sewing machine, indicated how a dream of savages holding spears inspired him to make an eye at the point of the sewing needle; Dmitry Ivanovich Mendeleyev (1834–1907) had a vision of the periodic table in a dream; and Friedrich August Kekule (1829–1896) visualized the benzene molecular structure as a snake biting its tail in a dream. Are they not co-creators or re-creators of the spiritual world?

---

[6] For the development of spiritual organs, please see references to essays and discussions on spiritual science in Ch. I, pp. 7–11.

[7] A person having occult or psychic ability is sometimes known as a *sensitive*. See for example, Sugrue, *There is a River: The Story of Edgar Cayce* [70].

[8] See for example, Steiner, *Autobiography* [69], and Smith, *The Burning Bush* [60].

The main themes of this chapter have been on the *more use, easier use* principle, on the holiness of our inner Self through re-creation and co-creation, and on the morphic fields of activities by which we experience who we really are. For our growth and development we shall further explore the relationship of Self-realization and Hallowed Be Thy Name in Ch. VIII.

III

Thy Kingdom Come

The word "kingdom" in "Thy kingdom" has many different interpretations. Events in *The Gospels* such as the resurrection of Christ, the return of Christ to his Father, the descending of the Holy Spirit upon the disciples during the Pentecost, and the Second Coming of Christ all pertain to "thy kingdom."[1] With these diverse meanings, it is no wonder that whether "thy kingdom" has come or not remains controversial.[2] In this book, which is about my personal reflections on *The Lord's Prayer*, I construe "thy kingdom" as the Christ Consciousness (same as the Christ Spirit), or simply *the Christ*. Since Jesus became the Christ after his baptism,[3] we may infer that the "kingdom," as the Christ Spirit, has come to Jesus. Jesus is a historical figure

---

[1] Please see Smith, *The Burning Bush* [60] for various interpretations of "thy kingdom."
[2] For example, even in *The Gospels*, we have "the kingdom of heaven is at hand" (*St. Mark*, 1:14'15, *St. Matthew*, 4:17); and "But if it is by the Spirit of God that I cast out demons, then the kingdom of God has come upon you" (*St. Matthew*, 12:28).
[3] According to *St. Luke*, 3:21–22, "the Holy Spirit descended upon Jesus in bodily form as a dove" when Jesus was baptised in the Jordan River.

and the Christ is the spirit in Jesus after his baptism. Likewise, the Christ is potentially in each of us waiting to be manifested.

Perhaps due to either ignorance or forgetfulness about Oneness, some of us have the illusion of being abandoned by our Father and yearn for His kingdom to come. Jesus uses parables to foretell this arrival of the kingdom. He foresees that it is more difficult for a rich man to enter the kingdom than for "a camel to go through the eye of a needle"[4] (*St. Matthew*, 19:24). For the multitudes, he uses the sower and the outcome of the seeds to illustrate his point (*St. Matthew*, 13:3–8). After the Mystery of Golgotha (the death and resurrection of Jesus), the seeds of the Christ are sown in us. Those who refuse the Christ completely would let the seeds fall on the path and be eaten by birds. Those who initially may be attracted by the teachings of the Christ but do not have the perseverance to practice them are like sprouting shoots that cannot take root because of lack of top soil. Those who would accept the Christ but have too many other diversions would not cultivate the Christ Spirit and let the tender shoots be choked by thorns. Only those whose seeds fall on good soil are the true Christians. Their seeds will bring forth grain manifold and they will let the kingdom come. The kingdom of heaven manifests like a mustard seed, and even though it is the smallest of all seeds, it will grow into a mighty tree and birds can build nests in it (*St. Matthew*, 13:31–32).

The Virgin Mary was chosen to birth Jesus. In *The Last Barrier* [25, pp. 90–92], Reshad Feild (b. 1934) recounts his Sufi teacher Hamid's eloquent exposition on the role of Mary. Hamid advises that we melt into Mary to let her gentle and sweet nature guide us to birth the Christ Spirit. We may regard Mary as the matrix of our bodies, the blueprint of life, and pray to her for help with our own birth of the Christ Spirit. If we recognize

---

[4]For various interpretations of this phrase, see http://eyeoftheneedle.net.

the purity of Mary and let the joy of life flow freely at every moment, then the Word will be manifested and there will be a reappearance of the Christ in the outer world.

It should be stressed that the reappearance does not come from our success in seeking the Christ *from without*. Rather it signifies only that when we are pure, the Christ, like seeds sown, will manifest in the outer world through our virtues. While we can eventually find God *as the Creator* if we investigate nature in its physical manifestation and refrain from any personal bias,[5] we cannot find God *as the Christ* from the physical side of the material world. St. Paul exhorts his congregation to strive for the realization of

Not I, but *the Christ in me*.[6]

In other words, to seek and manifest the Christ, we must search within using our spiritual capacities.

This approach is not unlike that of Taoists to realize the Light within the Golden Flower (see Ch. I, Fig. 1, p. 15 and discussions therein). When Christianity was first introduced into China during the Tang dynasty (618–907), some Taoists readily accepted its teachings and weaved the two traditions together (see Palmer, *The Jesus Sutras* [50]). This may account for the similarity of the two approaches to Self-realization.

Christ's sacrifice on the cross is a new kind of initiation for all human beings. Before Golgotha, initiates had to go through some kind of a three-day sleep ritual (such as the Egyptian temple sleep) in order to know and connect with the spiritual

---

[5] The recent emergence of many prominent scientists affirming their belief in the existence of God is illustrative of this assertion of Steiner. See for example, Cornelia Dean's article Faith, Reason, God and other Imponderables in the Science Section, Books on Science, of *The New York Times*, July 25, 2006.

[6] Italics added. This line was frequently used by Steiner to paraphrase St. Paul's words in *Galatians*, 2:20.

realm — to understand that they were more than the physical body and to learn what missions to fulfill on this earth plane. This "sleep" induced the equivalent of a near death experience or an out of body experience. Lazarus might be the last person recorded in *The Bible* to be initiated with this ancient ritual.[7] After Golgotha, everyone can, without going through the old ritual, connect with the spiritual realm via (the seed of) the Christ within. Recall that the Möbius band model clarifies the "no inside or outside" aspect of spirituality. So living in the Christ or letting the Christ live in us makes no difference, and either will enable us to reconnect with spirituality directly.

Those living in the Christ will emanate at least the following four virtues: compassion, courage, humility, and patience. In fact, similar virtues were emphasized in both Eastern and Western cultures even before the time of Jesus. The Chinese classic *I-Ching* states four inherent attributes of the CHIEN[1] hexagram (see Ch. I, Fig. 3, p. 21) which are procreating, prospering, benefiting, and persevering. Confucius (552/1–479 B. C. E.) expounds the CHIEN[1] hexagram and explains how such attributes would induce virtues of benevolence, civility, morality, and efficiency. Following the Greeks, some Christian traditions have practised the four cardinal virtues: prudence, temperance, fortitude, and justice. On the surface these three sets of virtues seem to be different, but I believe that the conscientious cultivation of any one set of virtues will consequently enliven the other sets. They are terms used to reflect the particular interests and emphases of human cultures at different times and places. Nowadays, it seems we are more inclined to resonate with terms of compassion, courage, humility, and patience, and so I will only concentrate on this set.

---

[7]Please refer to the essay Three Day's Journey in the book *The Burning Bush* [60, pp. 312–327] by Edward R. Smith for a brief history of initiation and in particular, the significance of Lazarus' initiation.

In *The Gospels*, there are many examples testifying to the compassion and courage of Jesus. He was often moved by compassion to heal the sick. He dined with the destitute and consoled the weak. He courageously defied the Sabbath and threw out the merchants from the temples. And what enormous courage and compassion he demonstrated by sacrificing himself on the cross for our sake! In recent times, Mother Teresa (1910–1997) answered the call from Jesus to found the Missionaries of Charity to service the poor, the sick, and the dying (see her book *Come Be My Light* [74, pp. 39–41]). Her life is an inspiring model of compassion.

The historical Buddha Gautama is a another model of compassion. When he attained Buddhahood he could have left the world. Due to his compassion he extended his stay for about forty-nine extra years to expound the Dharma, which he knew the multitude would have great difficulties grasping. Legend has it that he was so kind that he never even killed an insect. The Buddha once had a headache [51, pp. 119–120]. He explained to his disciples that this headache was due to karma incurred during one of his previous lives. In that life he was a boy in a fishing village. One day he saw two big fish tied to a pole under the hot sun and they were nearing death from heat stress and thirst. He laughed at them rather than felt compassion for them. When those fish later reincarnated and took revenge on the villagers, he only experienced a headache rather than being slaughtered because he was a Buddha.

Most of us are so entangled in our daily activities that sometimes it is not so easy for us to act benevolently. Therefore, sages have shared with us contemplative insights to help us generate kindness in our hearts. In Buddhism, the Bodhisattvas are enlightened beings who vow (see Trungpa, *Born in Tibet* [78, p. 56]) not to enter "Nirvana so long as a single blade of grass remains unenlightened." The Dalai Lama, who is deemed the incarnation of the compassionate Bodhisattva Avalokitesvara, has repeatedly taught us to generate compassion by imagining that all human beings have been our mothers one time or another in past incarnations. He points out in his book *An Open Heart* [28, p. 96] that to generate true compassion, we do not just imagine abstractly:

> We must use a real individual as the focus of our meditation, and then enhance our compassion and loving-kindness toward that person so that we can really experience compassion and loving-kindness toward others. We work on one person at a time.

In Tibetan Buddhism, *tonglen* is the meditation practice of "taking and giving," in which one concentrates on one's breath by inhaling all sufferings and exhaling all joys. One becomes compassionate by exhaling joys, and it takes great courage to inhale sufferings. Pema Chödrön (b. 1936), a Tibetan Buddhist nun and an American teacher on meditation, observes in *The Wisdom of No Escape* [7, pp. 57–64] that when one first starts practising *tonglen* one may have merely a thimbleful of courage, but after some time one may gain a teacupful; the practice will awaken one's heart and courage. [8] *Tonglen* is an efficient way to generate both compassion and courage, which are closely knitted and usually reinforce one another.

Like compassion and courage quickening each other, humility and patience also enliven one another. Let us look at some illuminative historical personalities.

The accounts of Jesus in *The Gospels* clearly articulate his great virtues of humility and patience. He tolerated his disciples'

---

[8]This practice can also help one become kinder and gentler toward oneself as well as others. Please see Trungpa, *Training the Mind* [81, pp. 26–35] for an in depth discussion of the practice.

ignorance of his purpose, taught people not to seek revenge or be angry even if being unfairly treated, washed the feet of his disciples at the Last Super, and allowed himself to be humiliated during his Passion.

Hui-neng (638–713), the Sixth Patriarch of Zen, recounts (see Cleary, *The Sutra of Hui-neng* [11, p. 89]) that the Buddha went out with his disciples to beg for his meals. He explains that the Buddha, with his accomplishments, did not really need to attend to ordinary chores of life himself but he did to show his ability "to humble his mind toward all people." When the Buddha was asked to expound the Dharma, he was ever so patient and gentle, illuminating different aspects of the Dharma to suit the diverse levels of awareness among his audiences.

Humility is highly valued in Chinese culture. Almost all of the sixty-four hexagrams in the classic text *I-Ching* are generally associated with mixed omens, some favorable and some unfavorable. The only exception is the hexagram [9] for humility or CHIEN [2], which forebodes no unfavorable omens. It signifies that humility would incur no calamities. The hexagram is made up of two trigrams, the upper one representing earth, and the lower one a mountain. A mountain is supposed to dominate above the earth, so the placement of its trigram in CHIEN [2] symbolizes the immense modesty of a sage for his willingness to hide his attributes and to act with humility toward others. The legendary deeds of the three sage kings, Yau, Shun, and Yu, are highly praised both by Confucians and Taoists. The kings were leaders of the people, yet lived humbly among them, and worked together with them to earn their livelihood in the fields.

Although many great teachers have inspired us to be humble, when the occasion arises, we very often fail to act modestly.

---

[9]For examples of hexagrams, including that for humility or CHIEN [2], see Ch. I, Fig. 3, p. 21. Humility is represented by the fourth hexagram in Fig. 3, and is not to be confused with the hexagram for CHIEN [1].

The practice of prostration in Buddhism is an effective way to cultivate humility. Steiner mentions another good way to cultivate humility. In *Life between Death and Rebirth* [64, p. 62], he suggests that we should bear the following thought:

> In the universal pattern it is of no importance whether something happens through us or through another person. ... One should not love something because one has done it oneself, but love it because it is in the world irrespective of whether he or someone else has done it.

He indicates that repeated contemplation of this thought would lead us to selflessness and humility.

Lao Tzu includes compassion and humility, and by implication also courage and patience, as two of his three cherished mottos for life:

> I have three gems, which I hold consistently: the first is compassion, the second is frugality, and the third is not daring to be the first in the world. Because of compassion I can be courageous. Because of frugality I can gain a broad view. Because of not daring to be first, I can have room for improvement.
>
> — *Tao Te Ching*, Ch. 67

Firstly, Lao Tzu considers courage as a consequence of compassion.[10] Secondly, he views frugality as a precious virtue to broaden our perspectives. Without frugality, our environment will be polluted with wastes and the resources of the earth will be deplenished at an ever accelerating rate. We should practice frugality earnestly and diligently.[11] Lastly, he stated that true

---

[10]So do the Tibetans as seen from the practice of *tonglen*.

[11]Recycling is one way to practice frugality. Its benefit is easy to see. We shall discuss further the principle of frugality in Ch. V, p. 82.

humility teaches us to learn with patience and strive for perfection, and thus be able to accomplish many things.

Many of us demand or expect others to immediately respond to and answer our requests. These tendencies are probably due to our mentality for self-importance. If we are less self-centered, we will not demand others pay tribute or attention to us, and then true humility and patience will emerge naturally. It is no wonder that great teachers are generally humble and patient.

There are many ways to foster the four virtues, and what I have stated is only the tip of these valuable teachings. I have not been able to live up to these high ideals. One has to prepare the soil before a seed can germinate and grow. Frequently reminding oneself of these teachings will help one resonate to the field of the Christ Consciousness with less resistance. Hence, one may eventually act in the spirit of the Christ with ease. This is the effect of the principle of *more use, easier use.*

Suppose we endeavor to cultivate these virtues. Would we then be living in God's kingdom? In the chapter titled **The Distressing Disguise of Suffering** of her book *In the Heart of the World: Thoughts, Stories and Prayers* [73, pp. 55–56], Mother Teresa tells a story which may reveal a profound aspect of the kingdom. It is about a nun in her order:

> After joining the Missionaries of Charity, this postulant had to go to the home for the dying destitute in Calcutta the very next day. Before she went, Mother Teresa told her: "You saw the priest during the Mass, with what love, with what delicate care he touched the body of Christ. Make sure you do the same thing when you get to the home, because Jesus is there in a distressing disguise."

When the nun came back three hours later she smiled beautifully and reported to Mother Teresa, "They brought a man from the street who had fallen into a drain and had been there for some time. He was covered with maggots and dirt and wounds. And though I found it very difficult, I cleaned him, and I knew I was touching the body of Christ!"

This postulant nun of Mother Teresa's order knew that Jesus is always in the distressing disguise of suffering because she was probably well aware of the mystery of the kingdom from the following biblical account:

> "... for I was hungry and you gave me food, I was thirsty and you gave me drink, I was a stranger and you welcomed me, I was naked and you clothed me, I was sick and you visited me, I was in prison and you came to me."
>
> Then the righteous will answer him,
>
> "Lord, when did we see thee hungry and feed thee, or thirsty and give thee drink? And when did we see thee a stranger and welcome thee, or naked and clothe thee? And when did we see thee sick or in prison and visit thee?"
>
> And the King will answer them,
>
> "Truly I say to you, as you did it to one of the least of these my brethren, you did it to me."
>
> — *St. Matthew*, 25:35–40

Interested readers may reflect on the story of the sister in light of this profound passage from *The Gospels* by following the four ways to understand a story, as advised by the Sufi master Sheikh Suleyman Dede (Feild called him Dede) [25, pp. 147–148]:

- literally, as an event;
- allegorically, as an illustration of something else;
- metaphysically, as an illumination of the great law of the universe; and
- mystically, as an experience by the heart for the truth within.

In summary, the cultivation of compassion and humility (and consequently, courage and patience) is a sure path to the realization of the Christ in us, and thus, THY KINGDOM COME.

IV

Thy Will Be Done on Earth as in Heaven

Most of us feel that this clause means we need to work hard on earth to complete God's will. However, a vision by J. J. Lynn (Rajasi Janakananda) (1892–1955) reveals that this may not be exactly the case. Lynn was a very successful business man from Kansas City, Kansas. He was the principal disciple of Paramhansa Yogananda (1893–1952).[1] His vision was reported by Sri Durga Mata (1903–1993), another disciple of Yogananda, in her book *A Paramhansa Yogananda Trilogy of Divine Love* [22, p. 140]. In this vision Rajasi heard voices of Jesus and Yogananda, together with his linage of masters.

On August 20, 1953, Rajasi was lying on the grass. He said, "In my heart and mind, I was calling out to the Masters, Babaji, Lahiri Mahasaya, Sri Yukteswarji, Master [Yogananda], and Jesus, when out of the ether all

---

[1] Recall from Ch. I (p. 13) that Yogananda's body remained uncorrupted for twenty days.

66

the Masters' voices in unison answered, 'I, of myself, can do nothing. Thy will be done.' "

This vision suggests that the spiritual realm would not interfere with our work in the physical world. It may inspire us but it will not force us to complete our will. Here, "Thy will" probably refers to Rajasi's intention to donate most of his assets to Yogananda's Self-Realization Fellowship Organization, but the process had not been finalized yet. Rajasi succeeded Yogananda, became president of the organization, and in May, 1954 gave it as a gift 22,000 shares of common stock of Kansas City Southern Railway, then worth more than one million (U.S.) dollars.[2] Rajasi did his will, following the message conveyed by the Masters, "Thy will be done."

We have discussed in Ch. I (p. 38) that we will reincarnate again and again on the earth plane. According to Rudolf Steiner, after the end of our present life, our souls will first briefly review the life we have just lived — most of those who had near death experiences have reported this brief life review — after which our souls will continue the review for an extended period of time.[3] Our souls will feel regret for our misdeeds and will be determined to atone for all the wrongs we did in the physical world. If we have lived a mostly virtuous life and have been beneficial to others, our souls may elect to continue to help others in our future incarnations.

With life reviews, we do not have to keep guessing at what God's will is for us in our next lives (and the present life) or how we are to comply with it. Indeed, Neale D. Walsch stressed in *Conversations with God, Book 3* [86, pp. 9–10] that God has given us freedom to decide what is best for us. The aspects of

---

[2] See http://ompage.net/Rajarsi/1955-02-21.htm.

[3] This period recovers the unconscious time one would have lost in sleep during the present life, and is roughly one-third one's lifetime.

God are being expressed through our best choices, which are the same as God's best choices for His Self. As discussed in the models of Intelligence, each of us may be viewed as part of the Sierpinski's triangle and the algorithmic generation of the triangle is seen as the process of how we together with God express His Self.

Notwithstanding, many saints and masters still would maintain the attitude that "Thy will" is God's will and not ours (or rather, theirs). They fully understand that we are all One and thus "Thy will" and "our will" coincide. Their humility and selflessness may provide the explanation why they would never regard their work as a personal will but as an aspiration to serve God. They will always strive for God's will to be done and only consider themselves as instruments for "Thy will."

Our best choices are made at the soul level. Depending on the clarity of our consciousness, our mind may not always know what we will at the soul level. When our mind is distracted or deluded by a myriad of desires, we may not always complete that will, or know why we are doing what we are doing. Enlightened beings teach us to calm our mind so we can become conscious of our true self and know the best choices. Only then can we complete our will as decided at the soul level and "our will," or equivalently "Thy will," be done.

If we are not always fully aware of our best choices, it will be difficult to know those choices of others. As a consequence, we all sometimes judge their *actions* superficially. Let me tell a short story that comically exposes this common shallowness.

> A madman escapes from home and runs out on the street. People from the house run after him hoping to bring him home. An observer who happens to be at the scene probably only notices that people are running and may not know that they are running for different reasons.

Metaphorically we are all running on the street. Some are deluded like the madman, running without any particular purpose and possibly inflicting sufferings to themselves or others. Others are enlightened, running and hoping to awaken the deluded. That is exactly what the Bodhisattvas are doing. According to Trungpa, *Born in Tibet* [78, p. 56], they vow not to enter Nirvana so long as there are still unenlightened beings as insignificant as a blade of grass.

The Chinese traditionally stress the attitude of *an-xin* in all their undertakings. Literally *an* means "to pacify" and *xin* means "the heart"; so *an-xin* means "to pacify the heart's urges." There is a Chinese idiom *xin-an-li-te*, which may be translated as: "When the heart is pacified, Tao will be gained." Acting according to the heart's urge is a way to be one with Tao. This is the Chinese approach to have "Thy will be done." This approach allows one to follow one's best choices, sometimes even without the mind's conscious knowledge of them.

But there is no fixed way on how to pacify one's heart. Let me use a Zen story to illustrate this point.

Two monks were sent back to their villages after completing their study from a Zen master. On the way they saw a corpse exposed in the open. One monk continued on his way without even taking another glance at the corpse. The other stayed behind, dug a grave, and performed appropriate burial rituals to appease the dead. Someone reported this happening to their master and wondered why they acted so strikingly differently even though both learned from him. The master replied that they both acted according to Dharma. One saw everything as void with nothing to fuss about; the other felt compassionate to help the dead rest peacefully. They both acted according to their hearts' urges.

Chuang Tzu (*c.*369–*c.*301 B. C. E.), an influential Chinese philosopher, was known for his eponymous book, which is full of stories illustrating his philosophy. One of these demonstrates that there may be different levels of *an-xin*.

> Chuang Tzu told his disciples that after his death, they should not bury him, not to mention elaborately. The sky would be his cover and the earth would be his resting place. But his disciples expressed their worry that if they did not bury the master's body but left it exposed, it would be eaten by birds of prey. Chuang Tzu replied that above ground his body would be eaten by birds of prey and underground it would be eaten by ants. He asked his disciples why they would favor the ants and not the birds.
>
> —abstracted[4] from *Chuang Tzu*, Ch. 32

If we were able to act in accordance with *an-xin*, then the cause and effect of our *actions* would not be of much concern to us. In reality, as the above stories illustrate, this is difficult, for there is neither a fixed way to pacify one's heart nor one single level of *an-xin*. It may be easier to arrive at *an-xin* from another Eastern view, through the simplified Hindu and Buddhist teachings of karma. Karma involves an elaborate theory about how our *actions* are causes and how their effects will be realized in the future (either in this life or future lives). In simple terms, the Law of Karma says that if we pay too much attention to the potential rewards for our *actions*, we are creating bad effects. Since we do not want bad effects, we can achieve *an-xin* if we do not fixate on rewards for our *actions*. From now on, we will designate this simplified idea of cause and effect as the principle of *action-reaction*.

---

[4]Abstracts are based on the Chinese original from *Chuang Tzu*. For the full story, see the translation *The Complete Works of Chuang Tzu* by Burton Watson, [88, pp. 318–319].

To explain the phrase "on earth as in heaven" in *The Lord's Prayer*, let's digress to investigate how the principle of *action-reaction* applies differently in the physical world than in the spiritual world. In the material world, *actions* and *reactions* are governed by the laws of physics. If we want to move our hands through the air, that would be relatively easy. The resistance of air is so slight that we almost do not feel it.[5] If we are to perform similar movements in water, we may feel we need to exert more effort because there is greater resistance in water than in the air. Should we try to move our hands through thick mud, it would be extremely difficult, if not impossible. In a denser environment we need to exert a greater force to accomplish an activity. We also feel that the bigger the force in our *action* the greater is the force of its *reaction*. This phenomenon occurs only on the earth plane. In the spiritual world, assuming we move with infinite speed and can complete any movement instantaneously, it will be as if there is no resistance whatsoever. Our *actions* in the spiritual world will create no reaction. In other words, the Law of Karma, or the *action-reaction* principle, does not hold in the spiritual world.

When we carry out "thy will" *on earth*, the principle of *action-reaction* implies that if the desiring force of rewards from our *action* is great, the karmic reaction force will be correspondingly great, resulting in great resistance and heavy karmic burdens; and if we let go and do not fixate on any reward, we will create less resistive reactions and hence fewer bad karma effects on earth. This may be why great masters advise us not to dwell on the results of our deeds. On the other hand, when

---

[5] According Newton's third law of motion, every *action* has an equal and opposite *reaction*. Here *action* and *reaction* are represented by forces. When a hand is moved through the air, the air is pushed away, and the air reacts to push the hand in the opposite direction with a force of equal magnitude. However, the effect (deceleration) to the hand is small because the hand is massive and dense compared to the air (Newton's second law of motion). Thus the hand moves through the air easily.

we carry out "thy will" *as in heaven*, the principle of *action-reaction* will not apply, and there will be no karmic burdens to *actions* in the the spiritual world. This is the ideal state Jesus suggests in *The Lord's Prayer*.

In Plato's *Phaedo* [53, p. 64] there is a section in which Socrates (*c.* 470–399 B. C. E.) discussed similar issues of the burden of our desires but with slightly different reasoning. Before his imminent death, Socrates explained to his disciples that the soul would be "contaminated" and "weighed down" by our physical desires. Only those who had "pursued philosophy in the right way," or in other words, developed their minds without any concern for material comforts, would go directly to God upon death. For those who had only pursued physical pleasures, their souls after death would "hover about tombs and graveyards" as ghosts.

In the Indian classic, *The Bhagavad Gita* [24, 18.12], it is stated (italics added) plainly that

> Those who are attached to personal reward will reap the consequences of their *actions*: some pleasant, some unpleasant, some mixed. *But those who renounce every desire for personal reward go beyond the reach of karma.*

This last statement is similar to Socrates' assertion that those with unpolluted souls go directly to God. Sri Ramakrishna [46, p. 82] compared performing worldly duties to breaking open jackfruits: one should first "secure the oil of divine love" to avoid being allured by worldly thoughts, just like one should first rub one's hands with oil to avoid getting smeared by the sticky milk of the jackfruit. Some teachers suggest we should treat materialistic desires with the same detachment as a swan feels about water: when a swan gets out of the lake after a swim, it has to shake only a little and all the water will be shed.

The great sage Lao Tzu advises us to complete our will with the ideal of *wu-wei*. The term *wu-wei* is translated as "non-action," which means neither "no *action*" nor "inaction." The Chinese character *wu* means "not having" whereas the character *wei* can mean either "an *action*" or "a purpose." In the days of Lao Tzu, people probably thought like many of us today. They mistook *wu-wei* as being passive or not doing anything. According to the Chinese classic[6] *Wen Tzu*, Lao Tzu emphasizes what *wu-wei* does not and does mean [12, Art. 124]:

> [*wu-wei*] does not mean that you cannot be induced to come and cannot be pushed away, do not respond when pressed and do not act when moved, keep stopped and do not flow, clench tight and do not let go. It means that private ambitions do not enter public ways, and habitual desires do not block true science. It means . . .

The practice of *wu-wei* in the sense that private gains should not come into public affairs is also deemed important in the West. In *The Hero with a Thousand Faces* [5, pp. 12–14], Joseph Campbell (1904–1987) demonstrates this point using the story in Greek mythology of the Minotaur, which we briefly paraphrase below:

> A majestic white sea-bull was sent by Poseidon, god of the sea, to Minos as a sign to enable Minos to claim the throne. Minos had promised to sacrifice the sea-bull back to Poseidon after he attained his throne. But he kept the beautiful animal in his herd and offered a substitute. His Queen was seduced by this white sea-bull and consequently gave birth to the monster Minotaur—a child with a human body but the head and tail of a bull. . . .

---

[6] *Wen Tzu* is a compilation of the teachings of Lao Tzu by Wen Tzu, whose identity has not been determined. Most quotes are taken from Thomas Cleary's translation [12].

Campbell comments that Minos had to bear responsibility and embarrassment, for he should not have "converted a public event to personal gain."

Lao Tzu also clarifies the meaning of *wu-wei* by contrasting the difference between acquiring knowledge and practicing Tao:

> Learning accumulates knowledge daily.
> Practicing Tao diminishes egotism daily.
> Keep diminishing until *wu-wei*.
>
> — *Tao Te Ching*, Ch. 48

When we study and learn a subject, we accumulate mentally a great number of facts about the subject. However, when we practice Tao, we gradually diminish our egoistic or selfish desires, become selfless, and ultimately no longer wish for personal gains. When *wu-wei* has been achieved, one is not deluded by selfish desires and is naturally in the state of one's true being; there is no need to "act out" an assumed persona or to conform to society norms. Lao Tzu teaches us that the latter "non-action" is accomplished by sages [12, Art. 17]:

> Therefore sages inwardly cultivate the arts of the Way
> and do not put on an external show of humanitarianism
> and dutifulness.

An example of how we can realize the comfort of our inner serenity even with our busy modern day lifestyle is evident in an article on the subject of vacation by Karen Robinovitz published in *The New York Times* [55]. She reports that many vacationers choose to deprive themselves of the usual travel extravagance and instead take a retreat in places with a very basic or rustic way of living where they seem to rediscover themselves or their priorities. Robinovitz quotes a comment by one vacationer, Dave Platter of Massachusetts: "It was suddenly a relief to not have to try to be anything for someone else." His experience indicates an appreciation of his inner comfort over any external vanity. Mr. Platter now does public relations work for the Shambhala Mountain Center.

The tradition of Hindu religion also teaches the ideal of *wu-wei* without using the term. The suggestion given by Krishna to Arjuna [24, 2.47] is very similar to Lao Tzu's advice. It stresses Self-realization via the path of selfless service, or *karma yoga*:

> You should never engage in *action* for the sake of reward,
> nor should you long for *inaction.*

By gradually diminishing our selfish desires and possessiveness, we will be emulating Heaven and Earth as expounded by Lao Tzu:

> Man follows the way of Earth,
> Earth follows the way of Heaven,
> Heaven follows the way of Tao,
> And Tao follows What Is.
> — *Tao Te Ching*, Ch. 25

Sages advise us to learn from the selflessness of heaven and earth and conduct our life likewise. By rendering selfless service to others, we would realize our true Self. Lao Tzu points this out succinctly,

> Is it not because he is selfless that he is Self-realized?
> — *Tao Te Ching*, Ch. 7

This conclusion is also echoed in the ending clause of the prayer of St. Francis of Assisi who shows us how to live so that "Thy will be done on earth as in heaven" (italics added):

> Lord, make me an instrument of thy peace. Wherever there is hatred, let me show love; injury, pardon; despair,

hope; doubt, faith; darkness, light; sorrow, joy. Oh, divine master, grant that I do not so much seek to be consoled as to console, to be understood as to understand, to be loved as to love. For it is in giving that we receive, in pardoning that we are pardoned, and *in dying to the self that we are born to eternal life.* Amen.

Indeed, this prayer is full of wisdom.[7] When we do others a service, if we harbor as our goal to gain eternal life or "get to heaven," then that deed would not lead to eternal life. This is the profound meaning of "in dying to the self."

In *A Search for Solitude: Pursuing the Monk's True Life* [43, p. 49], Thomas Merton makes a very insightful observation between a selfish and an unselfish person:

> ... Even when he eats and sleeps, an unselfish person is doing it for others. But even when a selfish man gives away his money and works all night for others, he does it for himself.

It is only through the complete surrender of any personal gain that in the end we can realize our Self. It is like a seed must die in order to manifest its true being as a tree. Stories abound that many sages passed away (and some were even aware of their imminent deaths) once they felt they had completed their missions.

The story of J. J. Lynn (Rajasi Janakananda), which we related earlier, is an example. According to Yogananda, his disciple Rajasi was an advanced Indian yogi in a former life. He was born to the West in this life as a successful businessman to assist Yogananda to procure financial stability for the Self-

---

[7]Motivational writer Wayne Dyer (b. 1940) has written a book, *There is a Spiritual Solution to Every Problem* [23], sharing his experience on living according to the teachings of this prayer.

Realization Fellowship Organization. Rajasi died shortly after
he endowed his assets to the organization.

In her book *In the Heart of the World: Thoughts, Stories,
and Prayers* [73, p. 88], Mother Teresa notes:

> Each of us is merely a small instrument; all of us, after
> accomplishing our mission, will disappear.

I think this aptly foretold exactly what happened: after she had
accomplished her mission to arouse our compassion to the plight
of the poor and the destitute, she simply "disappeared." Her
statement also applies to others. Let me illustrate this with the
story of Merton.

Merton had dedicated his whole life to be a true contemplative, and his mission was to write an authentic treatise
on contemplation. He had worked on and off on the subject
throughout his monastery years in Gethsemane, Kentucky. In
1947, soon after he became a monk and published his successful
autobiography *The Seven Storey Mountain* [40], he completed
a pamphlet called *What is Contemplation?* As he continued to
deepen his practice as a contemplative, he realized he needed
to rewrite this booklet. It was not until 1959, almost eleven
years later, that he had time to make extensive revisions. The
pamphlet became a new book titled *The Inner Experience.*
Somehow he still considered the manuscript incomplete. In 1967,
he created the Merton Legacy Trust to administer the literary
rights to all his unpublished works, and he specified that this
manuscript was not to be published. [8]

In the early spring of 1968 he was invited as a panelist at a
religious conference that would be held in December that year in
Bangkok. Before embarking on the trip he made minor revisions

---

[8]See the Introduction to *The Inner Experience* [45], or Merton's journals [42,44].

to the manuscript and in May, gave it to his former teacher and good friend Daniel Walsh.[9]   During the second half of 1968, Merton might have been aware subconsciously that he had accomplished his mission with the completion of this important work. However, his reasoning mind was not fully conscious of his own readiness. In his journal of that year he revealed in some entries an urge to disappear to an isolated place or to disappear from the earth plane. For example, in *The Other Side of the Mountain* [44, p. 148], on July 29, 1968, he entered: "But if I can find somewhere to disappear to, I will." And on October 15, 1968 [44, p. 205], he wrote: "I am going home, to the home where I have never been in this body ...."

It turned out Merton disappeared somewhat dramatically. Before the conference, he had traveled to Alaska, the West Coast, and then Asia to see his friends. At the conference in Bangkok on December 10, 1968, he presented a talk and his last utterance of the talk was, "So I will disappear." A few hours later he was found dead, electrocuted by a faultily wired fan (see *The Asian Journal of Thomas Merton* [42, p. 343 and p. 258]).

Unlike masters who are content to disappear after completing their missions, the unenlightened masses, like most of us, are not sure of their mission in life, and have strong attachment to their works, relations, and possessions. Sri Ramakrishna explained that it is like we are living in a room full of soot: no matter how careful we are, we cannot avoid getting some of the dirt. He also said that we are like children engrossed by their toys and games. After our explorative childhood stage, it will be easier for us to outgrow our toys and games. As we enter our mature phase of life, we will learn to practice Tao, achieve *an-xin* and *wu-wei*. Then THY WILL will always BE DONE ON EARTH AS IN HEAVEN.

---

[9] *Ibid.*

V

Give Us This Day Our Daily Bread

In order to carry out THY WILL, we need much resource. Naturally most of us will think we have to ask God to provide us our necessities. Nonetheless, it is only a misunderstanding that we need to pray for our provisions every day. As will be explained below, God has always given us our daily bread. Even before we ask, it is already given. This is a manifestation of the endowing aspect of Intelligence. The clause GIVE US THIS DAY OUR DAILY BREAD is intended as a prayer of thanksgiving rather than of supplication. If we are sincerely thankful for what we have, we would naturally be non-demanding and humble. In this chapter, we explore how to live in accordance with the spirit of this clause.

Let us first contemplate the implied meanings of the words "day" and "bread." "This day" stands for a period of time. It can be this life, this year, this month, this week, this day, this hour, or this moment; and "daily" may correspondingly be life after life, year after year, month after month, week after week, day after day, hour after hour, or moment after moment. Ordinary bread is nourishing but can go stale if not used in time. The "bread" in *The Lord's Prayer* does not have to stand for material things; it can be an opportunity, a skill, a talent, or a myriad of things.

There is a parable, abstracted below, about talents[1] in *St. Matthew*, 25:14–30.

> Before going on a journey, a man entrusted his three servants respectively with five, two, and one talent according to their abilities. When the man returned to settle the accounts with his servants, he found that the first two servants had doubled their amounts to ten and four talents respectively, while the third servant hid his one talent underground. The man took this third servant's one talent and gave it to the servant who already had ten talents.

In *The Burning Bush* [60, p. 139], Edward R. Smith explains that each of us is equipped with certain "talents" or skills for this earthly life, and these would progressively fade away for future lives if not fully used. On the other hand, if we use them appropriately, they would become more abundant in our future lives.

As stated above we may view our "daily bread" as skills or resources, which will be there for us always in a timely fashion. We may not be aware of this endowing aspect of Intelligence because of the materialistic conditioning of the human mind. It is my hope that when you have finished reading this chapter you will more fully appreciate this aspect and thus act in ways

---

[1] In this context, a *talent* is the wage for more than fifteen years of a laborer.

more conducive to your success. We will investigate how we can maintain a healthy attitude toward our "daily bread."

Recall that in Sierpinski's triangle model (Ch. I, p. 29), the empty space is pregnant with all possibilities. To emphasize the inexhaustibility of this bestowing aspect of the Void, Lao Tzu calls it *the Mystic Female*. He says,

> A sage does not hoard:
> What he does for others enriches him.
> What he bestows on others endows him more.
> — *Tao Te Ching*, Ch. 81

In his view, the more our skills and resources are used, the more will be created for our future use. There is no need to worry whether we have enough for tomorrow or even for the moment. If we hoard resources and stop giving them away, we are creating a thought form that we may not have enough; our reality will then become self-fulfilling. Thus a sage has no need to save or hoard. Observing a connection between greed and hoarding, Lao Tzu also advises:

> Do not prize hard-to-get items and you will not turn people into thieves.
> — *Tao Te Ching*, Ch. 3

Even though we may not have valuable items and we may not worry about thieves, it is prudent custom to protect our assets with risk management such as carrying insurance or making estate planning. We have maintained these practices to such an extent that the forces of their morphic field are too strong to effect a quick change. Society is probably not currently capable of changing its value system to follow the ideals of Lao Tzu. We may have to conform to custom, just as in driving we have to go with the flow. The following comment by Chang San-feng, the

Taoist master and a great teacher of *Tai Chi Chuan* (shadow boxing), is most relevant in our dealings in the world of today (see Cleary, *Vitality, Energy, Spirit* [18, p. 196]):

> Seek the same as other people, but do not be greedy like other people; get what others get, but do not hoard like others do. Without greed, there is no anxiety; not hoarding, there is no loss. One is like others in outward appearance, but the inner mind is always different from that of the worldlings.

When people care and respect the things given to them, they will naturally treasure and not misuse them. That may be the reason Lao Tzu regards frugality as one of his three gems. Based upon my own experience, teaching students in calculus classes solving optimization problems is one way to instill their appreciation of the principle of frugality. We witness nature manifesting this frugality via the optimization principle. For example, a soap bubble will appear naturally in a spherical shape so as to minimize its surface area and maximize its volume. Beehives are hexagonal so that beeswax is used efficiently.

The Way of Tao encourages us to seriously practice frugality and attempt to eradicate, or at least moderate, our wasteful habits. Nowadays most of us practice some form of resource recycling. Nevertheless, we shall have to continue to challenge ourselves to be more innovative in the practice of frugality so that we can modestly (but not extravagantly) sustain our collective human lifestyle.

Assuming our "daily bread" is always provided for us, we would not worry about whether our bread will materialize. The point is how to minimize our unnecessary worries and be efficient, that is, to be in the state of *non-ado*, whence we are alert and prepared, but not fretful or worrisome.

The non-ado attitude does not mean we need not make an effort to accomplish an activity. For example, faced with a full table of delicious food, we still need to pick the food up and put it into our mouth. Indeed, were the food to fly into our mouth, we still would have to open our mouth to let it in, and then chew, swallow, and digest it. Even though we do not have to worry about the outcome, we may not accomplish our goals without preparation. If we feel we are not yet up to some task, it is probably not yet the time to tackle that activity. It is not productive to just wait for events to unfold (let alone be impatient). Imagine a toddler yearning to drive a truck. Would its parents grant such a wish? While waiting to complete whatever we seek to do, it may be beneficial to us if we do not remain idle but continue to hone our skills for our eventual endeavor. A Buddhist proverb sums this up nicely, "The teacher will appear when the student is ready."

Let me use the activity of respiration to illustrate why we can really live without much ado in the present. When we breathe we simply inhale and exhale without paying attention to how we breathe. Normally we do not need to deliberately expand the lungs or draw in the diaphragm. Generally, we do not have to worry that there may not be enough oxygen for respiration. The air permeates our environment even before we inhale. Breathing is just one of many activities illustrating that, even before we act, all that we need is already provided. When referring to respiration, non-ado is also identified by stillness, especially during meditation (see below). By the *as above, so below* principle we shall understand that all our undertakings are well equipped for us and by being in the state of non-ado, we will simply be doing what we intend to do at the moment.

The Eastern practice of meditation, especially deep meditation, emphasizes certain aspects of respiration. Exploring in detail this practice will enhance our appreciation of the non-ado attitude when we learn to infuse it into our other activities. During meditation, we concentrate on breathing, observing its inhaling and exhaling, without forcing them. We are reminded to only pay attention to the present breath — neither the previous one nor the next one. We are always in the present.

Practitioners in deep meditation seem to have ceased breathing. The breath is so subtle that there appears to be no breathing through the nose. The air is coming and going within an area near the navel and is flowing freely with the body's natural rhythm without interference. The mind and the breath are resting on each other, but it does not mean a person in that state neither thinks nor breathes. It is the state of non-ado or perfect stillness, when the mind is completely calmed without erratic thoughts because it is concentrating on breathing. In Buddhism, this state is called *mindfulness*. In Taoism the practice is called *womb breath*, because it is like a fetus breathing through its mother in the womb, without itself working. However, this non-ado/stillness state is not yet the state of *Samadhi*.

Samadhi is the state of uniting with God or "melting" into God.[2] It is difficult to articulate fully such an experience. Nonetheless, some masters use metaphors to hint at how one may feel when one is at that state. According to esoteric teachings, before reaching *Samadhi*, the kundalini energy, or the *chi*, which is held to lie coiled at the base of the spine, will have moved up to the third eye *chakra* (the point between the eyebrows) and then to the thousand-petal lotus *chakra* (the top of the head). The state of non-ado/stillness may or may not lead to *Samadhi*. Attainment of the latter depends on the grace of God and cannot be forced, though it can be nurtured. For example, Sri Ramakrishna was frequently in that state.

---

[2]It is the same as the state of Cosmic Consciousness, or the clear light state.

Studies and reports indicate that many others have experienced *Samadhi*. The feeling of intoxication is often a special aspect of this divine experience. *The Rubáiyát*[3] is a collection of poems, written originally in the Persian language and attributed to the Persian mathematician, astronomer, and poet, Omar Khayyám (1048–1123). Yogananda, who authors *The Rubaiyat of Omar Khayyam Explained* [90],[4] regards *The Rubáiyát* as a passionate praise about this spiritual state and in the Introduction, [90, p. XVI], he notes the role of wine:

> In plain fact, Omar distinctly states that wine symbolizes the intoxication of divine love and joy.

The Chinese Taoist Ancestor Lu Tung-pin also writes about the experience in a poem known as the *Bai-zi Bei* [Hundred Character Tablet] and says it is similar to "Having drunk the wine of longevity, ..." (see [18, p. 85]). In *Further Along the Road Less Traveled* [52, p. 138], M. Scott Peck (1936–2005) reports that Carl G. Jung once communicated with one of the co-founders of Alcoholics Anonymous and postulated that alcoholics might have greater thirst for the spirit. In view of the state of *Samadhi*, this may not be an unreasonable postulation.

In my own meditation practice I have never experienced *Samadhi* and am extremely far from the state of non-ado or stillness. Nevertheless, by understanding the process, I have been inspired to act with less fuss and to appreciate the importance of full attention to the task at hand.

We should be careful to distinguish between non-ado/stillness and *inaction* or laziness. In the state of non-ado/stillness one is living in the present fully aware of the situation — one pays complete attention to one's breath. If one is inert and lazy

---

[3] *Rubáiyát*, derived from the Arabic root word for "four," is an iambic pentameter quatrain with a rhyme scheme *aaba*.
[4] The alternative spellings for Rubáiyát and Khayyám in this book title are original.

then one may miss many chances to use one's talents in time. As mentioned earlier, to be in the state of non-ado/stillness is to be alert and prepared, but not be over-reacting, fretful, or worrisome. It is a state of the mind rather than a state of the physical body. During meditation, when one is in the state of non-ado/stillness, one is neither asleep nor drowsy but in a heightened state of consciousness (in Buddhist terms, *fully awake*). One is lively, energetic, and ready to tackle any task.

The central teaching of Zen Buddhism is about how to become enlightened, or *fully awake*. Buddhism maintains that everyone has Buddha nature. (The model of Sierpinski's triangle sheds light on this aspect.) However, we may not be aware that we are born with Buddha nature, just like we may not be aware of the Christ Consciousness in us. We need to learn how to realize, cultivate, and maintain this hidden Buddha nature and that means to become enlightened.

Buddhism emphasizes "activating the mind without dwelling on anything." [5] For example, if one fixates on attaining Buddha nature, one may never succeed. When one happens to realize it but dwells on keeping it, one may just lose it. It is most beneficial to us if we can maintain this attitude of non-dwelling in all our undertakings. Recall Steiner's advice to his student who was developing his spiritual organs in Ch. I (p.10): "not to think about this." This subtle practice, which requires that we are aware of our intent yet not to fixate on it, is sometimes difficult to explain clearly. The Zen traditions are rich with stories and koans illuminating this point.

The following story about how a Zen student cares for her mind is a typical example. Before enlightenment, she sees a mountain as a mountain and a stream as a stream. Her mind is

---

[5] See Cleary, *The Sutra of Hui-neng* [11, pp. 11 and 108], and Cleary, *The Secret of the Golden Flower* [16, 8.36].

deluded by the material manifestation. To seek enlightenment, she has to kill this deluded mind and negate all material cravings. Thus she sees a mountain not as a mountain and a stream not as a stream. She understands that everything is emptiness and all phenomena are mind created, or *mayas*.[6] But after enlightenment, she again sees a mountain as a mountain and a stream as a stream. She realizes that if she dwells on the newly gained enlightened view and keeps on negating material cravings, she would be in another kind of fixation and another kind of illusion. So after enlightenment, she appears to live not differently from an ordinary person — except that she knows why she sees a mountain as a mountain whereas an unenlightened person does not even know the view of a mountain is an illusion.

The difference between an awakened master and one who is still on the path seeking enlightenment can be exemplified by that between the verses[7] of Wo-lun and Hui-neng. Wo-lun was regarded as an accomplished Zen master (though in fact he wasn't) and had written a poem about his enlightened state. Hui-neng was the Sixth Patriarch of Zen, and he once heard his students recite the poem by Wo-lun:

Wo-lun has a skill.
He can cut off hundreds of thoughts.
His mind is never aroused by the environment.
Bodhi[8] grows day by day.

On hearing this verse Hui-neng explained to his students that if they practiced according to this verse of Wo-lun they would become fixated on cutting off thoughts and would be still in illusion. So he composed another verse for them to practice:

---

[6] *Maya* is a Sanskrit word meaning (an) illusion.
[7] See Cleary, *The Sutra of Hui-neng* [11, p. 59]. The translations are adapted from those of Cleary's.
[8] *Bodhi* means perfect wisdom or enlightenment.

Hui-neng has no skills.
He does not cut off his thoughts.
His mind is aroused by the environment repeatedly.
How can Bodhi grow?

Hui-neng did not want his students to fixate on only one idea, even if it is the idea of enlightenment. On another occasion he explained to his audience [11, p. 21]:

If you do not think at all you will cause thoughts to be stopped entirely. This is dogmatic bondage. This is called a biased view.

Masters will not dwell on anything. Buddhist teachers usually advise their students to use the "ordinary mind" to face all situations. Therefore one sees a mountain as a mountain and a stream as a stream.

This point of non-dwelling on anything is also taught by Lao Tzu (see the classic *Wen Tzu* [12, Art. 131]) who outlines the consequence of fixation in a more practical fashion:

Sages do not want anything and do not avoid anything. When you want something, that may just make you lose it; when you try to avoid something, that may just bring it about.

Neale D. Walsch clarifies the reason in *Conversations with God, Book 1* [84, p. 11]:

You will not have that for which you ask, nor can you have anything you want. This is because your very request is a statement of lack, and your saying you want a thing only works to produce that precise experience — wanting — in your reality.

He attributes this phenomenon to a function of our *controlling thought*, also called the *Sponsoring Thought* [84, p. 12]:

> ... because the Sponsoring Thought behind every supplication is that you do not have now what you wish. That Sponsoring Thought becomes your reality.

Please note that a fleeting desire or wish would not put us immediately in the binding state. Only when we dwell or fixate on this idea of want (or don't want) does the idea become a Sponsoring Thought, which in turn becomes our reality. The mantra "activating the mind without dwelling on anything" would be a very useful advice to train us not to be bound by our desires. Our intent or wish is like a little bird. Once we make a wish we should let it fly away to work for us so that it may return and bring back to us what we desire. Our desires are spiritual activities like Tao, and they always return. If we chain the bird and do not set it free we would only have that bird hovering over us: we would never get our wish fulfilled.

When we pray for something, the request must have been on our mind for a while but not yet fulfilled. Our continued longing turns into a fixation which becomes our Sponsoring Thought and reality. We are bound into a state of continuous "desire for that something" which is equivalent to a state of not yet getting it. Therefore, dwelling on a desire only creates the state of non fulfillment of said desire. [9] If we *persist* in wanting something to appear, then it will just *resist* appearing. I would like to coin the phrase *persist-resist* to remind us to be careful not to fixate on our desires. Walsch, commenting on the desire to resist earthly passion, writes ([84, p. 100], italics original), "*What you resist persists. What you look at disappears.*" This is an example of

---

[9]St. Teresa of Avila also observed this truth and said [72, p. 143], "If we try hard to grasp everything, we lose everything."

persist-resist applied to the act of "resisting earthly passion." In this sense, *persist-resist* and *resist-persist* refer to the same principle.

Let me first expand on the *persist-resist* principle with a personal but probably common experience. I have occasionally misplaced an object and have had to look for it. Either it is found in a few attempts or its presence simply eludes my detection. In the latter case, I become so frustrated that I stop the search reluctantly and turn to do something else. Just when I occupy my mind with something else the missing object will appear serendipitously. I have experienced this in my daily life time and again, and found that the *persist-resist* principle may provide an explanation. When I *persist* in looking for a missing item, a Sponsoring Thought fulfills my "desire of finding it" so the item will *resist* appearing to me. But as soon as I stop the search and attend to another activity, I am no longer bound by this Sponsoring Thought. The reality that the missing item does exist somewhere ensures a chance for the item to attract my attention and be found without further effort.

Here is another common experience explainable by the *persist-resist* principle. Very often when we try hard to recollect something, say a name, a phrase, or a word in a crossword puzzle, we just cannot recall it; however later when we are in a relaxed mood, it may spring up in our mind out of nowhere.

Allow me to relate another personal story to illustrate the *persist-resist* principle. I was awarded a grant for a project. Within ninety days of its expiration, I had to submit a final report signed by a supervisor. The grant allowed me to hire a consultant to advise me on my project as well as to help prepare the final report. Thus after the grant expired, I expected the consultant to send me a well-prepared report early so that I did not have to revise it and could have the supervisor sign it without rush. Alas, he was too busy to work on it. At regular intervals during the ninety-day period, I sent the consultant additional information to facilitate his writing of the report and reminded him to complete it on time. About two weeks before the deadline he told me that the report was ready and he would mail it to me. I kept checking the mail and it never came. Then, in the afternoon on the Friday prior to a Monday deadline, his secretary faxed me a copy of the report. On examining it, I realized that I could not avoid a revision. I had to make several minor changes, retype the report during the weekend, and rush to get an official signature on Monday.

Well, I should have known better. The *persist-resist* principle was working against me without missing a beat. Maybe due to the morphic field effect, I was still entrapped in my old habits. I was not able to activate my mind carefully enough, and I still fixated on my wants and don't wants a great deal.

Stories abound about how seekers endeavored to become enlightened but experienced getting nowhere. As they took a break or were distracted by other minor acts, they suddenly became enlightened. Afterwards, many wrote verses to commemorate the moment of their enlightenment. In Zen traditions, such accidental enlightenment is called *attaining sudden insight.*

As an example, there is a well-known poem by a Zen nun who was "looking for the spring season," which is a metaphor for her quest for enlightenment. In her poem, she lamented that she had spent all day in the mountains to search for the spring season. Even with her straw sandals worn she had found no sign of it. Upon returning home, she smelled the fragrance of plum blossoms and realized that spring was already fully present among the plum branches.

Students of Taoism keep searching for the Mystic Female on the way to master the celestial secret. Most Taoist teachers are unable to fully articulate the Way of Tao. However, a Taoist adept Chen Xu-bai (1278–1368) understood that the

Mystic Female and its related alchemical terms are essentially metaphors. He wrote a treatise **Compass Center Directions** [18, pp. 165–176] explaining the role of non-attachment as the essence of Tao. He predicted that after practitioners had read his book, their search experience for the Mystic Female would be as described in his coda:

> *Treading till my iron boots were worn, I don't know where I can find it. Now it comes to me without any effort.*

These stories or the little bird metaphor can serve to alert us not to *persist* in getting something. If we learn to educate ourselves about this *persist-resist* principle with simple incidents such as looking for missing objects, then by means of the *more use, easier use* principle we will gradually complete all our tasks without being hampered by the effect of the *persist-resist* principle. In other words, we will be progressively more adept at "activating the mind without dwelling on anything."

When we activate our mind with less dwelling, we are more likely to achieve what we desire. That may be why prayer chains often help others miraculously whereas prayers for one's own wishes are less successful. When praying for others we are more relaxed and less anxious but when praying for oneself, one is more wound up. Anxiety affects the ability to relax and intensifies the fixation on what one prays for.

Having seen the utility of the *persist-resist* principle under various situations, we may wonder why sometimes, even when we have tried not to fixate on our desires, we still can't have our wishes fulfilled. I suspect the reason is that most events that happen are overdetermined. There may be friends and family members praying and making well-intended but unwitting wishes on our behalf, or opponents and foes wishing us failure and bad luck, or the highest self willing some outcome unbeknownst to our conscious mind. With so many different factors influencing our activities, it is hard to attribute causes to effects. Lao Tzu gives the following advice: [10]

> I cannot repel the occurrence of misfortune. I trust myself not to attract misfortune. I cannot compel the presence of fortune. I trust myself not to relinquish fortune. Since I am not the cause of my misfortune, I do not worry when I am at rope's end. Since I am not the cause of my fortune, I do not brag when I have it made.

Chuang Tzu relates a story (more correctly, parable) involving Confucius [88, pp. 318-319] that exemplifies this statement of Lao Tzu.

> Confucius was confined in the wilderness by an army. His enemies wanted to capture him for their king. Confucius and his disciples had been surviving for seven days on only wild vegetables. Despite being in such a dire situation, Confucius was seen singing, accompanying himself on his musical instrument. After expounding on the virtues and Tao, Confucius told his puzzled disciples that he admired how the pines weathered a snowstorm and that he considered himself fortunate to have this opportunity to strengthen his virtues like the pines.
> —abstracted from *Chuang Tzu*, Ch. 28

Chuang Tzu comments that worldly fortunes come and go like the seasons, and they should not affect one's serenity. This parable shows that non-attachment to circumstances and outcomes is the best attitude in life. Whatever we do we should do it with the ideal of *wu-wei*, which we discussed in Ch. IV (pp. 73–75).

---

[10]This passage is a translation by William Sit; for Cleary's translation, see [12, Art. 52].

Let me retell a story from *The Gospel of Sri Ramakrishna* by M. (Mahendranath Gupta) [46, pp. 648–649] about a pious weaver and how his attitude of non-attachment helped him remain calm and thankful in calamity.

> After work, the weaver was studying scriptures when some robbers broke in and snatched him to abet a robbery in town. The robbers forced the weaver to carry some loot. Suddenly the police arrived. The robbers escaped. The police brought the weaver to the judge. Recognizing the weaver, the judge asked why he was brought here. The weaver replied that by the will of Rāma[11] he was studying the scripture, by the will of Rāma he was forced to abet the robbery, by the will of Rāma the police arrived, and by the will of Rāma he was taken before the judge. After hearing his explanation, the judge released him. On his way home, he told his friends that by the will of Rāma, he was released.

This weaver has the perfect attitude of non-attachment to circumstances and outcomes. He understood that he did not actively seek any occurrence. Every event just happened to him. He was happy that he could serve Rāma's will and be his instrument.

During the writing of this manuscript, by the will of Tao, something relevant happened to me that helped me understand the comic nature of events.

It was two days after a great snowstorm in the Northeast. My husband and I had to use the car that evening. Snow was pushed by plow trucks to the curbside of streets and so piles of snow blocked the entrance of most driveways, including ours.

---

[11]Rāma is an incarnation of Vishnu, an aspect of God. See Ch. I, p. 17 and also the section on the trinity aspect of God, starting on p. 16.

That afternoon, I went out and tried to shovel some snow but really could not get much done. I noticed that there was a team of sanitation workers clearing snow. Some were even shoveling snow at the curbside by hand. One worker on the opposite side of the street and I happened to notice each other and exchanged smiles as if acknowledging our tedious tasks. Then I wondered if he would come over to help me. He seemed to have read my mind. Help he did offer. He asked a plow truck to come and shoved all the snow away to clear the entrance and the surrounding area of my driveway. I thanked him and went inside.

Two hours later, I took a peek outside. Well, the worker who had helped me and his team were gone. Another team of workers had pushed snow from other parts of the street to our spot and our driveway was blocked with even bigger piles of snow! By the will of Tao, my husband and I had to shovel a great deal of snow before going out.

These stories indicate that sometimes things do happen to us without our active participation or conscious anticipation. This clause of *The Lord's Prayer*, GIVE US THIS DAY OUR DAILY BREAD, suggests that we always be thankful for our experiences, live calmly to attain the non-ado/stillness state when consuming our "daily bread," and nurture the *wu-wei* attitude when utilizing our "talents" in our activities.

The famous pianist Artur Rubinstein did live his life to the fullest in this fashion, as attested by his two autobiographies *My Young Years* [56] and *My Many Years*.[57]. He was generous enough to share with us his observations of this wonderful aspect of life [56, p. 478]:

Providence, Nature, God, or what I would call the Power of Creation seems to favor human beings who accept and love life unconditionally. And I am certainly one who does, with all my heart. So I have discovered as a result of what I can only call miracles that whenever my inner Self desires something subconsciously, life will somehow grant it to me.

Truly if we can attune to Tao unconditionally, events may just happen easily without our struggles. Life will be like the wonderful ride down the Yangtze rapids depicted by the famous poet Li Po (701–762):

Before the wails of apes along the river banks died down,
Our light boat already sailed past ten thousand mountains.

VI

And Forgive Us Our Trespasses as We Forgive Those Who Trespass Against Us

This clause advises us to seek forgiveness from Our Father if we have sinned and to be forgiving if we have been hurt. The Bible (*St. Matthew*, 6:14–15) tells us that we will be forgiven if we forgive others. St. Francis of Assisi said, "It is in pardoning that we are pardoned." [1]

However, there are deeper and subtler meanings of forgiveness, and we should explore this clause more fully. We have mentioned earlier that we are to use our highest thoughts to experience the grandest version of who we are (Ch. II). Certainly, our peace and happiness are enhanced when we are willing to

---

[1] See Ch. IV, p. 75, for Assisi's complete prayer.

forgive transgressors, and it is not because we have to please God or others, or to have our sins forgiven that we forgive others, but rather we need to attain *an-xin* — to be at peace with our inner Self. The primary reason to forgive is for our own well-being.

One reason that we sometimes judge ourselves so harshly is that we cannot forgive ourselves. We hate what we have done yet do not have the courage to face up to the reality required to facilitate a change. Loving kindness toward oneself is just as important as it is toward others. Only one who has a clear conscience with self-respect can act with compassion and forgiveness. We may discern that some of the discussions below on forgiving and not hating others may also apply to the self.

Imagine that our original mind is like an ocean or a mirror. It can function best when the ocean is calm or the mirror is clear. When we feel we are being wronged or when we scheme to commit immoral acts we become astir like waves in the ocean or dust covering the mirror. We lose our clarity and peace. We become very miserable, like ants on the lid of a boiling pot. As soon as we stop these unhealthy thoughts we are able to clear the mirror, calm the ocean, and become peaceful and happy again.

According to Buddhist teachings, when we dwell on an agitated state of mind, we are metaphorically trapped in the wheel of the six paths (or worlds). These six paths are among ten spiritual realms that are indications of our states of existence:

- The *path of hell*, where the perpetual fire of rage is dominant;
- The *path of hungry ghosts*, where greed and insatiable cravings are dominant;
- The *path of beasts*, where stupidity and stubbornness are characteristic;
- The *path of asura*, where pride and egotism are characteristic;

- The *path of the human*, where judgment and reasoning are characteristic; and
- The *path of celestial being*, where indulgence in pleasure is dominant.

Staying in such worlds only prolongs our suffering. We should aspire to reach the other four states of existence:

- The *path of learning*, where one seeks for truth;
- The *path of realization*, where one understands sufferings and truth;
- The *path of Bodhisattva*, where one helps those who are suffering and aspires for enlightenment; and
- The *path of Buddhahood*, where one is completely enlightened and free from delusion and sufferings.

As we delve deeper into the meaning of forgiveness we shall see that the path of Buddhahood will lead us toward THY KINGDOM COME (discussed in Ch. III), where kingdom represents the Christ Spirit that exemplifies the four virtues: compassion, courage, humility, and patience.

Now, let us see what Jesus teaches us on the practice of forgiveness. Jesus suggests how we can forgive those who have wronged us. He advises:

> Do not resist one who is evil. But if anyone strikes you on the right cheek, turn to him the other also; and if anyone would sue you and take your coat, let him have your cloak as well; and if anyone forces you to go one mile, go with him two miles.
>
> — *St. Matthew*, 5:39–41

In our litigious society today, it seems that only very naive people would follow such advice. If someone strikes my right cheek, not only will I protect my left, I will go to the authorities and demand the aggressor be punished. If the court does not rule in my favor, I would claim that justice has not been rendered and there must be some kind of conspiracy. When we feel we have been wronged, our first impulse probably spurs us to react as above. But is this the best kind of reaction for all concerned?

Let us consider our usual response when we learn that a crime has been committed. We surely sympathize with the victims and their affected families. However, we may also feel some empathy toward the offenders as we listen to verbal attacks being launched against them by their victims. The reason for this empathy is that we sense that the victims are filled with hate and rage. Their unforgiving attitudes serve to reinforce the mental anguish that they feel.

Yes, when people feel that they have been attacked or violated, their first reaction may be anger and revenge. This reaction harms them in three ways:

- Firstly, whenever they recall the incident with hate and anger they will experience the hurt again mentally (remember the morphic field effect);
- Secondly, when they spend time and energy to plan a vendetta, they deplete their health and well-being; and
- Thirdly, if they actually carry out their plan they will be destroying their "goodness" and "wholeness" just as the aggressors did.

When people decide not to forgive they will not feel happy or peaceful even if they win in court. But the moment they are willing to forgive the offenders, they will feel a great burden lifted from their heart and will immediately regain peace of mind.

When we look into the matter more closely, we understand that nursing the wounds with revenge and hatred only hurts our inner Self even more — we are unwittingly blurring our mirror with more dust and rousing our ocean with bigger waves. Notice how our feelings are uplifted if we hear forgiving statements made by the offended party. We would know then the wounds for all concerned would start to heal.

Dr. Gerald G. Jampolsky (b. 1925) recounts in his book *One Person Can Make a Difference* [36, pp. 13–30] a true story of one Zalinda Dorcheus, who forgave the killer of her son. He chronicles how Dorcheus, after many years of deep hatred, struggled to come to terms with herself by truly forgiving the killer, and the difficulties she had to overcome. Dorcheus had to actually experience the awful effects of hate to understand the art and importance of forgiveness. Finally, she became awakened and said [36, pp. 26–27]:

> I was destroying myself through my hate and bitterness. My body was falling apart, and it seemed to me that the hate inside me was attacking my own body.

Her experience with hate echoes exactly what Thomas Merton writes about self-hatred and its variants in his book *New Seeds on Contemplation* [41, p. 73]:

> It destroys and consumes the self that hates, and not the object that is hated. Hatred in any form is self-destructive, and even when it triumphs physically it triumphs in its own spiritual ruin.

People who are unforgiving and fill themselves with deep hatred may wish and believe that transgressors will go to hell upon death. This may be why a statement[2] like "Hitler went to heaven" becomes quite controversial. But what is hell? After

---

[2] Neale D. Walsch's *Conversations with God, Book 1* [84, p. 61], *Book 2* [85, pp. 35–36].

death — after discarding the physical sheath — the soul will be in a state of pure consciousness. In other words, after death everyone will be in heaven (Ch. I, p. 2). Suppose after death, the soul still has physical cravings and there is no physical body to help it quench them. Then it will experience "hell." It may need "time" [3] to adjust to its new state of existence before realizing that it is futile to cater to carnal cravings. This may be the case especially if before death the soul has strong materialistic desires. "Hell" is thus a "temporary" state of consciousness when the soul aches to fulfill its insatiable carnal desires. [4] Recall in Ch. IV (p. 72) we quoted Socrates' explanation that polluted souls are weighed down by physical desires, while those who pursue philosophy in the right way go directly to God. God is always in heaven because He transcends such desires. Most of us need to overcome them "gradually."

As difficult as it might be for people with hatred to comprehend, the soul of a transgressor as hideous as Hitler might "achieve" heaven after death "ultimately" if it can overcome its carnal desires, and this does not depend on the wishes of haters. Indeed, the haters may find peace of mind themselves if they forgive.

The attitude of forgiving is not inborn and needs our conscientious cultivation. The Dalai Lama tells us that we definitely have to make an effort to nurture forgiveness. He suggests that we may treat those who hurt us as our teachers and every trespass as a stepping-stone toward becoming a more compassionate being. He advises us to thank our transgressors for their willingness to create bad karma for themselves in order to help us progress. This teaching is demonstrated by the following well-known Buddhist folklore about Buddha Gautama.

---

[3] In this discussion, "time," "temporary," "gradually," and "ultimately" are words inapplicable to the spiritual world but are used to enhance our understanding of "hell."
[4] According to Walsch [85, p. 36], God told him, "... hell does not exist."

As the legend goes, in some previous life before Gautama became the Buddha, he met a sage who knew that Gautama would become Buddha in a future life. This sage not only wanted to witness the event but also facilitate his progress by being his teacher in that future life. So during the life when Gautama was to become the Buddha, the sage incarnated as his cousin Devadatta and became an antagonist of Gautama. In this role, he provided great challenges and multiple opportunities for Gautama to realize his Buddhahood. Devadatta was later swallowed alive by "hell" because of his evil deeds. Nonetheless, he would eventually attain Buddhahood himself.

In *The Vipassana Dipani; Or the Manual of Insight* [47, *Kanakacchapa-Sutta*], Ledi Sayadaw[5] (1846–1923), a Burmese Buddhist, recounts the lesson Buddha Gautama taught his disciples that it is far more difficult to be reborn as a human being than the yoking of a turtle. There was a blind turtle, swimming randomly in an unfathomable ocean, and then there was a yoke adrift in this ocean. Gautama asked whether it might be possible that in the course of time the yoke arrived at the precise place and time where and when the turtle put up his head, and yoked on to it and told his disciples that while such an occurrence is extremely unlikely, it is a thousand times harder to obtain "the opportunity to become a man again by a man who has expired and is reborn once in any of the four realms of misery."

The simile is intended to show us that a reborn is unlikely to be merely by chance and that we have to earn it by performing good deeds and abstaining from doing bad ones (a very difficult feat, but we are given the opportunity).[6] Not only are we not born by chance, all the people we encounter in life are similarly not by chance. It is not just a happenstance or coincidence that we meet someone.

---

[5] For his biography, see http://www.ubakhin.com/ledi/biograph.htm.
[6] See Ch. VII, p. 121, for an exploration of why we are born here repeatedly.

According to Walsch [85, p. 176],

> ... every person who has ever come to you has come to
> receive a gift from you. In so doing, he gives a gift to
> you — the gift of your experiencing and fulfilling Who
> You Are.

Dr. Gerald Jampolsky, whom we mentioned earlier, relates
a touching story in his book *Love Is Letting Go of Fear* [35,
pp. 100–101] that clearly exemplifies this point. Dr. Jampolsky
is a famous psychiatrist who practices in California and has
appeared on national TV programs. A young man watched the
doctor on TV and felt something special about Jampolsky's
eyes that compelled him to immediately hitchhike from Virginia
to California. He came to the doctor's office, sweating, and
insisted on seeing him. When asked by Dr. Jampolsky what he
wanted, he was at a loss. Neither knew why he was there. At
the suggestion of the doctor, they meditated together. Then
Dr. Jampolsky heard an inner voice saying,

> "This man came across the country as a gift to you to tell
> you he saw perfect Love in your eyes — something that
> you have difficulty seeing yourself. Your gift to him is to
> demonstrate total acceptance to him, something he has
> never in his life experienced."

Then he embraced the young man.

The compassion in Dr Jampolsky's eyes was recognizable
even through a TV screen. The young man went to the doctor
to receive the gift of loving human contact. The doctor received
a gift of experiencing and fulfilling his true being.

We have discussed the undesirable effects of hate and
illustrated the fact that every happening is not accidental but
rather is a blessing in disguise. Jesus teaches us to appease

transgressors. We should not view the act of appeasing as weak and cowardly. Quite the contrary, only those with tremendous inner strength can act in that way. One has to be really humble, courageous, and compassionate in order to avoid contention with others. If we are humble we will not feel so easily offended. If we are courageous we will not be afraid of aggressions from offenders. If we are compassionate we will not only be forgiving but also pray for the awakening of our transgressors so that they may understand that aggressions will only result in damaging their own inner Selves.

Lao Tzu says,

> Those who do not contend will have no one in this world
> contending against them.
>
> — *Tao Te Ching*, Ch. 22

If people are satisfied and do not strive to gain any fame or material possession, naturally they would not compete with anyone for anything and consequently no one can compete against them. In that case they would experience few conflicts and much peace. Such practice requires tremendous self-discipline.

Great masters emphasize the importance of self-discipline in their teachings. In the book *The Sutra of Hui-neng* [11, p. 66], Hui-neng tells that he sees the excesses and errors of his own mind but not the right and wrong or the good and bad of other people. Confucius stresses that one should criticize oneself squarely, but treat others with leniency. The Taoist expert Liu I-Ming uses the symbol ⊡ consisting of a square inside a circle to represent aspects of Tao.[7] Alternatively, the symbol can be applied to illustrate the above Confucian ideal behavior: Inwardly, we should be like a square with right angles, very

---

[7] "Merging with the ordinary world, harmonizing illumination" (see *The Inner Teaching of Taoism* [14, p. 305]).

exact and honest, but outwardly, we should be perfectly round, smooth, and equable.

Let us see how two other ancient teachings on self-discipline and an observation on grudges help us understand the true meaning of forgiving. Confucius says,

> Do not do unto others what you don't want others to do unto you.
>
> — *The Analects*, 15:24

As recorded in the classic *Wen Tzu* [12, Art. 52],[8] Lao Tzu advises us:

> To pursue *actions* that cannot be criticized, but not to resent other's criticisms. To cultivate *actions* worthy of praise, but not to expect other's praise.

Lao Tzu further observes that,

> After deep grudges have been reconciled, residual grievances are unavoidable.
>
> — *Tao Te Ching*, Ch. 79

Forgiving deep grudges is like healing deep wounds: scars will inevitably remain. Whether we forgive or are forgiven, the aftertaste of bad feelings still lingers. By the above teachings, what hurt us should inspire us not to act with aggression in turn. It is far better that we be critical of our own actions so we will commit no transgression and thus minimize grudges against us. When we forgive, seek no revenge, and decide not to hurt others (including our transgressors) but to help them, that is true forgiving. Thus, we progress and transcend from the reactivity of forgiveness to the activity of benevolence.

---

[8]Translation from Chinese original by William Sit.

As a constructive advice to practice benevolence, Confucius says:

> Whatever stand the self wishes to take, first help others take their stand; whatever position the self desires to reach, first help others to reach their position.
>
> — *The Analects*, 6:30

Here "stand" represents the location one may occupy during ceremonial rites, which are important events in life, and only high officials can stand in prominent places. "Position" may represent the high esteem or expertise one may acquire in one's career. Generally, many would aspire to a prominent stand and a high position. The sage suggests that we help others achieve their aspirations before fulfilling our own. This suggestion is sometimes referred to by a shortened Chinese phrase, literally, "Establish others, empower others," which may be translated as: "Help others reach their goals."

Jesus teaches us this Golden Rule:

> ...whatever you wish that men would do to you, do so to them; ...
>
> — *St. Matthew*, 7:12

This Golden Rule, well known since antiquity, may also be presented as "Do unto others as you would have them do unto you." It complements the mottos of Confucius (*The Analects*, 15:24 and 6:30). However, one should not expect one's good deeds to be reciprocated because of the *persist-resist* principle we explained in Ch. V (pp. 89–92). These teachings are not the means to obtain what we want — they are vehicles to enlightenment and Self-realization toward THY KINGDOM COME.[9]

---

[9] Kingdom is interpreted as the seed of our higher Self or the Christ Consciousness in Ch. III.

We all realize deep within us that what we want will also be what others want. Ideally we should take the initiative to help others achieve their goals. This high ideal has always been the main tenet of the Confucian school. The poet-politician Fan Zhong-yan (989–1052) of the Sung dynasty put this eloquently,

> Before anyone under the heavens cares, I care.
> After everyone under the heavens rejoices, I rejoice.

Fan had experienced first-hand the tragedies of wars and empathized with the sufferings of common people. As a good government official it was natural for Fan to help his people attain a life of peace and sufficiency before he thought of his own welfare. We recall from Ch. III (p. 59) that the Bodhisattvas have a similar ideal to help others — they would not enter "Nirvana so long as a single blade of grass remains unenlightened." Nowadays, these ideals may seem unreachable to many of us. Nevertheless, we should remind ourselves of these teachings and strive to be as compassionate as possible. By the *more use, easier use* principle, one day we may act with compassion as automatically as we breathe.

We need to beware of a subtle aspect when we help others. We should not help others to the point that they rely completely on us and lose their incentive for personal growth and Self-realization. To become Self-realized, they have to work hard at improving themselves. No one can do this work for them. We may, however, endeavor to provide resources and opportunities. Let me briefly recall a parable of the ten maidens from the Bible (*St. Matthew*, 25:1–13).

> Ten maidens were waiting for the bridegroom until midnight. Five who were wise had their flasks filled with oil for their lamps and five who were foolish had not. While waiting, the unprepared five ran out of oil and

begged the wise maidens to share some of their oil but were refused. They had to go out to get oil and thus missed meeting the bridegroom.

In his book *Further Along the Road Less Traveled* [52, p. 97], Dr. M. Scott Peck, commenting on the parable above, makes an insightful observation. He notes that had Jesus been just teaching us compassion or forgiveness he would have made the maidens share the oil in this parable. Peck reasons that the oil has a deeper meaning and is a symbol for our preparedness. In his view, each of us has to do our own preparation; others cannot do it for us — there can be no sharing. We can share all our material resources but we cannot share our own growths and preparedness. This is analogous to our thirst; someone can guide us to the fountain or even bring water to us if we are too weak, but no one can relieve our thirst by drinking the water for us — we have to drink the water ourselves. We have to cultivate our own spiritual growth so that when the bridegroom (Christ Consciousness) comes we are well prepared to receive him.

In our discussions on forgiveness so far, we began by observing that hate in any form hurts our inner being. Next we learned from Buddhism how we can practice forgiveness by regarding our enemies as our teachers. Then we explored the attitude of true forgiving, which inspires us to discipline our behavior and to practice the Golden Rule. Now, we are going to explore that the realization of Oneness with God will awaken in us our commitment to forgiving and benevolent acts.

The teachings of forgiveness and benevolence have been around for thousands of years, and we are frequently reminded about them by masters all around us. Yet some people don't seem to be able to practice these teachings with enough commitment. I suppose the reason may be that they view themselves as separate entities and do not realize that they are connected

as One. If they understood that they are all One, they would
not hurt or blame *this Oneself* and would work for *Its* well-
being. It is like the hands would not hurt the feet by prevent-
ing their ability to walk, or the stomach would not blame the
mouth for eating too much. Recall the circle model of God
(see Fig. 8(b) in Ch. I, p. 34). The projected points in the circle,
no matter how close they are with one another, are always
separate. Only when the points are directed inward along the
radii do they all approach the same center. So looking within,
we shall realize that we are all one with the same Godhead,
Christ Consciousness, or Buddha nature. In *The Gospel of Sri
Ramakrishna* [46, pp. 201–202], Sri Ramakrishna explains,

> Fully awakened souls are beyond virtue and vice. They
> realize that it is God who does everything.

He then tells a story, paraphrased below, that shows this point:

> A monk while on his way to get alms saw a landlord
> beating a man. He tried to stop the beating but
> was instead beaten unconscious by the landlord. He
> was then brought back to the monastery. He regained
> consciousness after another monk poured milk into his
> mouth. Asked who was giving him the milk, he replied
> that the one who had beaten him was now feeding him.

However, he comments [46, p. 172] that it is not easy for us to
become fully awakened when life depends entirely on food. Our
food dependency preconditions us to identify with our body,
to have a tendency to look without rather than within, and
subsequently to not perceive that we are all One with God.

According to esoteric cosmology, human evolution is divided
into five long ages and we are currently emerging from the Dark
Age (the fourth age) and perhaps entering a new age that is

sometimes referred to as the Light Age.[10]   Sri Ramakrishna
lived toward the end of the Dark Age from 1836 to 1886. He
helped people learn compassion and see the *Oneness* in them as
a preparation for the Light Age.

According to Steiner's esotericism (anthroposophy), this
preparation started as early as some time before the last third of
the Dark Age — approximately at the beginning of the Current
Era. Around that time, there happened a single event — the
Mystery of Golgotha—which endowed us with the Holy Spirit
or the Christ Consciousness. Since then, some have found
enlightenment and are able to perceive that we are indeed all
One. By the end of the Light Age, hopefully more will become
enlightened. The Future Buddha Maitreya will come and lead a
multitude to a more spiritual and compassionate way of living. It
was only during the Dark Age that human beings gradually lost
contact with the spiritual realm and became almost exclusively
focused on the material plane. Now, as we are entering the
Light Age, there are more and more enlightened people around
to awaken us to connect with the divine spirit.

During the Light Age, our consciousness will brighten and we
will become more aware of our spirituality and Oneness. We are
like that slumbering princess in *The Sleeping Beauty*, waiting
to be awakened by a prince. Even our material world may be
reflecting the dawning of this Light Age. If we look around we
can find many translucent or transparent manufactured goods.
For example there are lights shining inside electronic mice and
lights in the soles of some sneakers. There are partly transparent
ballpoint pens and many completely clear plastic containers.

---

[10]The Hindu names for the first four ages are: Satya Yuga or Krita Yuga, Treta
Yuga, Dvapara Yuga and Kali Yuga. The exact span of each age and hence their
dates vary widely depending on the cosmology chosen. In *The Burning Bush* by
Edward R. Smith [60, p. 623], the Dark Age spans five thousand years from 3101 B. C. E.
to 1899 C. E., and is followed by our age which began from 1899 C. E. See also
http://en.wikipedia.org/wiki/Yuga.

There is extensive use of glass in the architectural designs of modern buildings.

These are the manifestations of the as spiritual so physical aspect of the *as above, so below* principle. As inwardly we become less dense, outwardly our material world will also demonstrate similar subtle changes to become transparent. Using the *as above, so below* and the *more use, easier use* principles, the human race may progress to a period when people realize that we are all One with God. Henceforth the more enlightened public will practice true forgiveness and benevolence in accordance with the Golden Rule.

VII

Lead Us Not into Temptation, but Deliver Us from Evil

Some people may be perplexed by the existence of temptation and evil. I suggest that following the perspectives of Eastern philosophies may provide the starting point to deal with temptation and evil.

In *Tao Te Ching*, having introduced Tao in the first chapter in exactly fifty-nine Chinese characters, Lao Tzu discusses immediately the duality in our world in the second:

Everyone recognizes beauty as beautiful.
This is due to the presence of ugliness.
Everyone recognizes goodness as good.
This is due to the presence of badness.

Thus the have and the have-not produce each other,
The difficult and the easy complete each other,
The long and the short shape each other,
The high and the low lean on each other,
Tone and sound harmonize each other,
The front and the back follow each other.

— *Tao Te Ching*, Ch. 2

The placement of this passage in *Tao Te Ching* shows that Lao Tzu recognizes the significance of duality. He uses common pairs of opposites to illustrate not only their contrasting polarity but also to emphasize their complementary nature. Lao Tzu explains that goodness and badness, beauty and ugliness, etc., pairwise coexist at all times in the external relative world. One cannot exist in the absence of the other. It is just a matter of perspective that we consider one dominating and the other subdued. In *Wen Tzu* [12, Art. 59], Lao Tzu reiterates:

When praise appears, then censure follows along;
When good appears, then evil comes along.
Profit is the beginning of harm;
Fortune is the forerunner of misfortune.

We are familiar with this sequencing and often observe that after something reaches the top, it comes down; or after it bottoms, it rises again. Those who observe the stock market have certainly seen this phenomenon.

In physics, examples of duality abound. Let us look at two such examples from mechanics. When a force is applied to a spring, the spring will be compressed or extended, and an opposing force of equal magnitude is generated, resisting the change. A stone that is tied to a string and flung around will stay in a circular orbit because a centripetal force pulls it toward the center while at the same time a centrifugal force of equal magnitude pushes the stone away from the center. In the world of duality, every event and occurrence will follow this rule.

In Ch. I (p. 6), we mentioned a light exhibit by physicist Arthur Zajonc, demonstrating light could not be perceived if there were only brightness — it can be seen only when there is something dark under illumination. The dual presence of brightness and darkness is essential to the perception of light.

Chuang Tzu expounds in an essay titled **Autumn Floods** [Autumn Waters] [88, pp. 175–183] the concept of relativeness through an imagined dialogue between the River God and the North Ocean:

> After the autumnal rain the river is teeming with water. The River God beams with pride at its magnificence. But when the river meets the enormous North Ocean, he is astonished by her immensity. He engages the North Ocean in a philosophical discussion and learns that nothing is absolute. Depending on the circumstances the universe can be considered small and the end of a hair can be considered big.
>
> — abstracted from *Chuang Tzu*, Ch. 17

Chuang Tzu declares in this essay that there is simply no absoluteness in this world of duality. Duality is stressed in *Conversations with God* [84, p. 22]: "In the absence of *that which is not*, that which IS, is *not*." [1]

The existence of duality allows people to have preference. Lao Tzu notes that they may show personal preferences for beauty and goodness, and antipathy for ugliness and evil. He observes [12, Art. 89] also that they consider the pleasant as right and the unpleasant as wrong — their search for right is only a search for

---

[1] Italics and caps original.

those who agree with them, and their departure from wrong is a departure from those who oppose them. However, in *Tao Te Ching*, he states very clearly that Tao has no subjective preference for one over the other and people should follow Tao by cultivating an unbiased view toward these dualities.[2]

> Heaven and Earth have no preference.[3]
> They regard all things as straw dogs.
> Sages have no preference.
> They regard all people as straw dogs.
> Isn't the space between heaven and earth like a bellows?
> It is empty yet inexhaustible.
> The harder it is pumped, the more it produces.
> More listening[4] or frequent probing,
> Neither is as good as staying in the middle.
>
> — *Tao Te Ching*, Ch. 5

Straw dogs were used in ceremonial rituals. They occupied important roles during the ceremony and were produced with care. Nonetheless, they were discarded afterwards. Both Heaven and Earth treat every object in the material world the same way — as straw dogs. A big tree and a small worm are both created with equal care and ingenuity, and neither Heaven nor Earth would favor one and condemn the other. Each is allowed to live and realize its true being, and when the time comes even

---

[2]The Maha Ati teachings in Tantric Buddhism share a similar view. When one is in the Maha Ati state, one simply transcends good and bad. See for example Trungpa, *Mudra: Early Poems and Songs* [80, pp. 22–24]. See also discussions on the beating of the monk in Ch. VII, p. 110.

[3]The phrase describing Heaven and Earth in Chinese is, literally, "not humane." Some writers translate the phrase as "unkind," "ruthless," "non-sentimental," or "indifferent." If we read the whole passage we should discern that "unkind" and "ruthless" do not fit the concluding message of the paragraph. Since being non-sentimental and indifferent would imply having no preference, I choose to translate the phrase as "no preference."

[4]Here we follow the Ma Wang Tui version where the original Chinese character for *words* (言) in traditional versions of *Tao Te Ching* is replaced by one for *listening* (聞).

a big tree will decay just as a short-lived worm will. We are the projections of the Godhead onto the space-time continuum (recall this is one of the circle models, Ch. I, Fig. 8(b), p. 34). Whether we are virtuous or evil, or somewhere in between, we come onto the world stage to experience and engage in our activities. We are all actors in a play but do not belong to the play. Even though each of us may play a different role, the hero and the villain are of equal importance during the show. After our per-formance we will leave the stage. In this sense, we are all straw dogs.

While Heaven and Earth have no preference, nature still provides. Lao Tzu compares nature in between heaven and earth to the empty space inside a bellows, which provides abundance for whoever works it. To Lao Tzu, further debates or probes about heaven and earth may confuse people or convince them to gravitate toward either pole. It is better to stay "in the middle." The character for "middle" in Chinese, besides conveying the idea of central, neutral, or without bias, can also be interpreted as "empty," meaning void of contents and in particular, void of preference. Striving to be in the middle in the world of duality is called *practicing the middle way*. We will later explore more fully the practice of the middle way in other traditions and at other times as well.

In Hindu culture, there are similar portrayals of the non-preference aspect of the Divine. The Divine Mother Kali is portrayed in M. (Mahendranath Gupta), *The Gospel of Sri Ramakrishna* [46, p. 9] as having four hands: the lower left hand holds a severed human head, the upper left grips a blood-stained saber, one right hand offers boons to her children, and the other allays their fear. These diametrically opposing features are to remind us Kali has no preference. The Divine Mother can give blessings but she may take them away, too. It is not up to us to value one and resent the other — for all is her play.

The Divine Mother Kali is regarded as the *Mahamaya*, the Great Illusionist. The world we live in is an illusion created by her. Thus, we should remind ourselves that all dualities are illusions set up to enhance our experience in the physical world. Indeed, we are reminded daily of an illusion by a very prominent event. We observe the sun moving across the sky and speak of sunsets and sunrises; in reality, we know it is the rotation of the earth that produces this illusion of the sun moving. Despite our knowledge, we seldom consciously consider this observation an illusory event.

A similar illusion is the phases of the moon as observed on earth. However in reality, it is due to the relative positions of the moon and the earth that we sometimes see a new moon, a full moon, or a half moon. The moon is always there fully round and the sun is always shining on it. During one full moon mid-autumn night Su Tung-Po (1036–1101), a famous poet of the Sung Dynasty, missed his far away brother and lamented:

> People experience sorrow, joy, parting, and meeting. The moon experiences darkness, brightness, waxing, and waning. This world has hardly been perfect since antiquity.

Su saw the waxing and waning of the moon with various degrees of fullness as a reflection on people's happiness and suffering. However, he remained *an-xin* with the hope that, despite being thousands of miles apart, he and his brother would both stay healthy and be able to celebrate the beauty of the moon.

Life is full of ups and downs. Yet many people only desire good fortune and cannot tolerate misfortune. We especially wish that our sons and daughters attain great prosperity. On the occasion of the birth of his son, Su Tung-Po wrote of a desire that reflects most Chinese parents' sentiment: "I wish my son to be dumb and clumsy, without sickness or incidents, and promoted to a high office." Here, Su invoked the Chinese traditional belief that great talents would attract jealousy, even from the heavens. In a true yet sarcastic manner, he observed that those with great wisdom appear dumb and those who are skillful seem clumsy. Many Chinese parents choose to give their children petty nicknames like "doggy," or "baby-shrimp." By emphasizing the lowliness of their kids, they hope that their children will not attract dark forces, can be easily brought up in good health to adulthood, and attain good fortune. Unfortunately, this son of Su passed away at a very young age, and there has been no evidence that this traditional practice brings prosperity to the offspring. If parents persist invoking their wish each time a child is addressed by his or her nickname, then their wish may resist to materialize (recall the *persist-resist* principle in Ch. V, pp. 89–92). The best attitude is to follow the advice of Lao Tzu in [12, Art. 131] (see Ch. V, p. 88): "Do not want anything and do not avoid anything."

Buddhist teachings frequently explain that the *original mind* (Buddha nature) functions like a mirror— it reflects every object appearing in front of it but retains no image of the object when the object is gone. The Buddha nature will not reject any circumstance or fixate on any encounter. On the other hand, the *intellectual mind* is so much occupied with likes and dislikes that it often overshadows the Buddha nature. Instead of allowing events to run their course and experience them as they are, be they successful or failing, sorrowful or joyful, the intellectual mind tries to push away the unpleasant and/or lingers on the pleasant. If we can tame these urges of the intellectual mind and restrict its principal function to that as an intermediary between the original mind and the outside world, we may learn to transcend any misery we think we are experiencing. Ideally, we should not over-indulge in our happiness either. We should not struggle with what happens to us but enjoy it to enrich our life.

One may wonder, if we cannot tame the urges of the intellectual mind and if values in this world, materialistic or not, are always relative, whether it would be better to choose death and enter the world of the Absolute for eternal bliss immediately. What would be the reasons to stay here to endure illusory duality? Do those who commit suicide make a wise or foolish choice?

It is natural to ask another question before we attempt to address the suicide problem.[5] The question is: Why do we exist? If we trace this question backward we may arrive at an answer somewhat like this: God out of His love creates us to share His glory. But then why does God exist? Why is there Life or Intelligence? In my research I have not been able to find out why there is Intelligence or God. God simply exists. One can study and understand part of the manifestations and functions of the Ultimate (as we have discussed in Ch. I) but one may not know *why* there is the Ultimate and *why* He created the universe. Great philosophers advise us to accept what It is rather than to ask why It is. The question "why do we exist" will lead us nowhere. To my understanding, our existence is a mystery that we have to bear while living on earth.

Back to the question: Should one end one's life abruptly? People are taught to value life preciously and not to commit suicide. The Buddha's metaphor of a turtle swimming into the hole of a yoke (see Ch. VI, p. 103) tells us that it is very rare to be born as human. By implication we should treasure this rare opportunity to realize "who we are." There is another reason other than "life is precious" why committing suicide is not a wise choice.

---

[5]Please note that the disappearances of the masters mentioned in Ch. IV (pp. 76–78), were not the result of self-inflicted suicides.

In his lectures *Life Between Death and Rebirth* [64], Rudolf
Steiner explains that after our death, not only do we lose our
physical body but we also lose our ability to rectify our many
wrongs or to fulfill our many desires. We earlier reasoned that
the spirit is moving at infinite speed and therefore there would
be no resistance to any *action*. *Action* and *reaction* are not
a phenomenon in the spiritual world. [6] For whatever *action* we
have undertaken in the physical, we are to experience its *reaction*
in the physical as well, some in the same lifetime and others in
subsequent ones. It would not matter whether the persons we
offended are still in the physical realm or are also "dead" and in
the spiritual realm. In order to remedy our misdeeds we must be
incarnated in a physical body and live in the world of duality.
In the Absolute we may only lament our earthly misdeeds but
may not alter our state of affairs before physical death. The
urges to correct our mistakes after death drives us to yearn for
rebirth. We have to be reborn to enact remedies.

According to spiritual science, the urge to be reborn is quite
dominant in the after life. We feel we are less than whole or
complete because of our selfish and immoral acts in our previous
lives. We desire strongly to atone for all our misdeeds to make
us whole again. We may feel we are bound by these karmic
debts and like to be rid of them and be free again. It takes the
help of highly developed spiritual beings in order to manifest
our wholeness through compensation in our next incarnation. [7]
We then make arrangements with more highly evolved spiritual
beings in "heaven" about what we intend to do in our next life
on earth. The clause THY WILL BE DONE ON EARTH AS IN
HEAVEN may be considered as a reminder. We are here on earth
to enact what we have willed in heaven.

---

[6]See also Ch. IV, p. 71, on the exploration of this viewpoint.
[7]See for example, Steiner's books: *Karma* [63] and *Life Between Death and Rebirth* [64]
for a detailed exposition of these ideas.

Suppose I am on the earth plane to carry out what I have "willed in heaven," yet somehow I lose the heart and courage to live, and I commit suicide. Then in my next incarnation, the new circumstances may not be as advantageous to work on my karma as my present life might have been. My earlier adversaries may not be reborn during my subsequent reincarnated life to allow me to reconcile my misdeeds. Had I been aware that I was not here by chance, that I had chosen willingly to be reborn in this world, and that many conditions had to be suitable in order for me to reincarnate and make amends, I would have striven to complete my life missions diligently and appreciated my precious opportunity to be living on earth. Ending my life prematurely on earth only postponed solving my problems, with possibly more difficulties in future.

That is why committing suicide should not be encouraged.

I hope this discussion will help people see how unwise it would be to prematurely terminate one's life on earth. If we cannot solve our problems alone, it is advisable that we seek help earnestly, rather than cornering ourselves in despair. We should remember that where there is a will, there is a way — a way we intended to participate in when we determined in heaven to rectify our karma. So it is not advisable to give up our life on earth before we fulfill our "wills."

Although there are depressed people contemplating suicide to end their lives, there are many more at the other end of the spectrum who want to enjoy every moment of life with gratification as well. We can truly live a happy and joyous life only if we understand that true happiness and joy rest "within" but not "without." Lao Tzu explains [12, Art. 41] that sages "use the inner to make the external enjoyable and do not use externals to make the inner enjoyable; therefore they have spontaneous enjoyment in themselves ..." We have demonstrated this point by noting that there are people who vacationed with deprivation (see Ch. IV, p. 74, where we discussed the article by Karen Robinovitz [55]).

Great teachers from every tradition teach us how to attain peace and calm in life. Teachings in Confucianism, Buddhism, and Taoism all stress the practice of the middle way. They may describe various methods with different nomenclature. The common denominator and goal of these teachings are to find our center under all circumstances so that we attain inner balance and outer harmony. In a sense it is to become *an-xin* (see Ch. IV, pp. 69–70).

Zisi (483–402 B. C. E.), the grandson of Confucius, articulates eloquently the relation between inner and outer:

> When joy, anger, sorrow, and happiness are not yet manifested, the state is inner balance; when activated in appropriate proportions, the state is outer harmony.
> — *The Doctrine of the Mean*, Ch. 1

Zisi does not ask us to be insensitive. He advises us to live authentically with our true being. There are many situations when we may simultaneously feel not just joyful but also sorrowful, not just angry but also happy. For example, we may feel sad that our child has to leave home to go to college, yet we are joyful for his movement into independence. We may be angered when a friend does not inform us about an awful event, but are grateful because she does that to protect us. When we balance our emotions we shall act with care to let these emotions emerge harmoniously and in proportion. The inner balance indicated by Zisi is a means to find one's center in the face of distractions or chaotic situations. It is like Goldie Locks trying out things in the house of the three bears to discover what suits her best.

Focus and caution are very important to the process of keeping the center or the practice of the middle way. It is like a toddler learning to walk: a little off center will make him topple. Zisi shows us some concrete ways to maintain our center. He emphasizes the importance of *shen-du*. The Chinese word *shen* means "be careful" or "be watchful" and *du* means "alone"; so *shen-du* means *be careful when alone*. Many of us would be careful when we are in public, but think that when we are alone we can relax and loosen somewhat. Zisi teaches us not to be that way. He writes,

> Nothing is more visible than secrets.
> Nothing is more manifest than trifles.
> So a man of noble mind practices *shen-du*.
> — *The Doctrine of the Mean*, Ch. 1

Why is that? Let us consider an example.

Occasionally, we learn that some prominent personality has a slip of the tongue. He has made some insensitive remarks in public, offending a certain group of people. Later he has to apologize that it is inappropriate for him to have made such comments. Why does he slip? Has he been careless? Well, obviously he has been careless during that particular incident. However, he may be even more careless when he is by himself. Had he been careful all the time even when alone, by the *more use, easier use* principle, his habit would enable him to be careful in public without much special effort. It is difficult for him to be always careful in public, probably because of his frequent carelessness when he is by himself. His most secret opinions would manifest sooner or later. In fact, if he were careful and understood that his biased opinion of others would not be acceptable in society, it would have served him better to search the origin of his bias in order to get rid of such prejudice. Thus he would never have to worry about offending anyone. This is the true intent of the phrase *be careful when alone* — to nip seemingly secret and unhealthy thoughts in the bud.

The Chinese classic *Shi-Ching*, also known as the *Book of Odes*, is a collection of over three hundred folk poems and lyrics from antiquity. The teaching *be careful when alone* may be illumined by one of its verses:

> Dare not fight a tiger empty handed;
> Dare not cross rapids just on foot.
> Obvious ones are easily seen;
> Subtle others are hard to glean.
> Be alert and cautious
> As if facing an abyss,
> As if treading on thin ice.
>
> — *Shi-Ching*, Bk. 6

We understand the inherent danger when we fight a tiger or cross rapids. We would instinctively be careful and prepare adequately for such an undertaking. However, conditions of false security in seemingly innocent endeavors are more difficult to discern. We should always be alert as if we are facing an abyss or treading on thin ice. A slight imbalance may bring disaster. We have to be watchful, but we also have to let go of nervousness somewhat. We have to locate the center so that, on the one hand, we acknowledge the dangerous situation, and on the other, release excessive anxiety and fear.

The teachings of Zisi on *be careful when alone*, of Lao Tzu on being without bias, and of the Buddha on being mindful,[8] are usually referred to as the teachings of the middle way. We are going to look at examples and teachings of other traditions and learn the significance of inner balance.

Pema Chödrön writes about her teacher Chögyam Trungpa Rinpoche in *The Wisdom of No Escape and the Path of Loving-Kindness* [7, p. 95]. Trungpa Rinpoche liked to create slight

---

[8]Please refer to Ch. V, p. 84 for a discussion of "mindfulness."

inconveniences in his surroundings. He "used to wear an obi, the wide belt that goes with a kimono, underneath his clothes, really tight, so that if he slouched, he would be uncomfortable — he had to keep his 'head and shoulders.'" He emphasized inconveniences as ways "to perk you up, keep you awake, present gaps in your cozy, seamless reality of centralizing into yourself." Trungpa Rinpoche shows us a way to practice being alert and centered. His approach to living exemplifies the teachings of the middle way.

In *The Way of Perfection* [72, p. 186], St. Teresa of Avila teaches her nuns the middle way by balancing the love of God and the fear of mortal sin:

> "Strive to walk with love and fear, and I guarantee your safety. Love will quicken your steps; fear will make you look where you are stepping so that you do not fall."

While the context in which St. Teresa's teaching appears is different from that discussed above, the idea is the same: strive for the middle with care.

Steiner talks about the importance of nurturing inner balance and outer harmony in a lecture series called *Esoteric Development* [65]. He says that for students who intend to develop esoteric abilities,[9] it is especially important to attain inner balance. He states that ordinary people would neither achieve great deeds of benevolence nor commit great harms of evil. Ordinary people do not distinguish the good from the bad that much in their activities, just as they do not see blue and yellow separately in the color green. On the other hand, students pursuing esoteric development can sense good and bad more distinctly, as if they can see blue and yellow separately at the sight of green. Ordinary people can see only

---

[9]Esoteric abilities are the functions of spiritual eyes and ears, see Ch. I, pp. 7–11.

the green shade from the rotation of the *Tai-ji-tu* (see Fig. 2, p. 20) while those with esoteric abilities can move with the *Tai-ji*, and hence are aware of its yellow and blue parts. They have more chances to perform endearingly benevolent acts, as well as greater temptations to commit devastating evil deeds. Steiner stresses that inner balance can quell their carnal desires to commit evil after they attain those abilities. Although Steiner's teachings mainly concern the esoteric students, they coincide also with those of the Eastern traditions and should be our ideal as well.

Let us examine the material and spiritual duality of our existence. In his exploration of spiritual science *The Influences of Lucifer & Ahriman* [66], Steiner concludes that there is, on the one hand, Lucifer, the Devil, who tries to lure us away from the physical world so that we attend *only* to spiritual matters and despise all material things; and there is, on the other hand, Ahriman, or Satan, who strives to trap us in the material world permanently so that we consider *only* things perceived by the senses and overlook spiritual influences. When Lucifer has the upper hand, we may be too spiritual, renounce the world as a mere illusion, and forfeit our physical evolution on earth. When Ahriman has the upper hand, we may become too materialistic, consider the sense world as the only reality, and neglect our spiritual development.

What is important is that we should strive to achieve a balance between the spiritual and the physical forces and not let either influence have the upper hand. We need not invoke, as Steiner did, the names "Lucifer" or "Ahriman." As discussed before (see the circle model of Oneness in Ch. I, Fig. 8(b), p. 34), we may regard humans as projections of the Godhead on the space-time continuum. We are revolving around the Godhead in circles. We may consider one influence as the centripetal force pushing us toward the center of the circle, which tempts us to become arrogant, to avoid performing any mundane work in the physical world, or to be like God. The other influence may be regarded as the centrifugal force pulling us away from the center of the circle, which instills in us an over-reliance on our senses and cleverness to disbelieve anything spiritual, and endeavors to trap us in the physical world. We should strive for a balance of the two forces. We have to be *in the world* so that we do not just attend to spiritual matters alone; yet we have to be *not of the world* so as that we are not trapped by our material existence.

The Gospels tell us that Jesus overcame the three temptations by Satan[10] and lived with great compassion, courage, humility, and patience. Metaphorically, we may say that Jesus kept his course on the circle, exemplifying his perfect balance between the two opposing forces by means of the Christ Spirit that lived in him since his baptism. The Christ Spirit is like a seed sown in us after the Mystery of Golgotha (see Ch. III, p. 56). So let us cultivate this seed within and let the Christ Spirit LEAD US NOT INTO TEMPTATION, BUT DELIVER US FROM EVIL.

---

[10] See Steiner, *The Fifth Gospel: From the Akashic Record* [68, pp. 130–137] for the significance of these temptations.

VIII

For Thine Is the Kingdom, the Power, and the Glory, Forever and Ever

Some versions of *The Lord's Prayer* do not include the clause FOR THINE IS THE KINGDOM, THE POWER, AND THE GLORY, FOREVER AND EVER. For example, the Catholic Church does not include this doxology in their version of *The Lord's Prayer*, but nevertheless it is sung during Mass. I regard this clause as the crowning jewel of the whole prayer. It reminds us to let the kingdom, the power, and the glory of our hidden Buddha nature or Christ Spirit radiate from us. That may be what Jesus means when he says (*St. Matthew*, 5:16), "Let your light so shine before men." For this to happen we should be as well prepared as the five wise maidens with enough oil for their lamps (*St. Matthew*, 25:1–13, see also Ch. VI, p. 108).

Intuitively, God's omnipresence implies that His kingdom, power, and glory will automatically last forever and ever. These attributes of God can be thought of as inherent in God's name. We may regard this chapter as an extension of Ch. II on the clause Hallowed be Thy name. How do we benefit from the teachings implied in this doxological clause? I would like to argue that the clause is meant to encourage us to emulate God in every aspect of our existence so we can also bring our "kingdom," "power," and "glory" (by which we mean, respectively, our *work*, *words*, and *virtues*) to eternity.

In ancient China, there was an essay about bringing our acts to eternity via three means: virtues, work, and words. For example, the three legendary kings of antiquity — Yau, Shun, and Yu — are highly praised for their great virtues. The Duke of Chou is esteemed for his dedication in establishing a prosperous and strong Chou Dynasty (1122–256 B. C. E.). Classics like *I-Ching* are treasured even today for their profound wisdom and inspiring teachings. The great philosopher Chuang Tzu [88, p. 32] describes how those who have achieved their eternal ideals may behave:

> A perfect person disregards self;
> A spiritual person disregards success;
> A sage disregards fame.
>
> — *Chuang Tzu*, Ch. 1

According to Chuang Tzu when one has attained the state of One with Tao, one will no longer seek immortality, achievement, or reputation. Chuang Tzu gives many examples of these saintly people in his eponymous book.

Let us see how these ideals are manifested in the acts of Jesus Christ. One virtue of a perfect person is his selflessness. He will sacrifice himself for the good of others. Jesus did exactly that by giving up his life on the cross. When a spiritual person ignores success it does not mean he does no work. Rather his work is not measured by material success. Because of his care for others and his focus on what he is doing, his work seems effortless to others who may not even realize that they are recipients of his benevolent efforts. The miracles of Jesus are certainly work of this nature. A sage with great knowledge does not seek fame. He simply lives with the common people and sets a good example. The Gospels abound in stories showing how Jesus kept company with the "sinners" and used parables to teach common people.

In *Come Be My Light* [74, p. 164],[1] Mother Teresa related that after she started working at the Missionaries of Charity, she suffered a "feeling of absence of God." Despite her prolonged suffering of this darkness, she continued in her commitment to serving the unfortunate. Her suffering sheds light on how a saint may disregard the self. Due to her total selflessness, she had complete empathy for those whom she served. Her soul was saturated with their despair and their thirst for God. We may consider her the personification of the Tibetan meditation *tonglen*[2] practice — breathing in all pain and suffering and breathing out all joy and happiness. When considering the life of Mother Teresa, we praise her unselfishness and her untiring dedication to the poor and the destitute. Her virtues are reflected in her work. Many are also influenced by her inspiring teachings.

Virtues are generally held in higher esteem than work and words, but in fact, there is no need to stress their differences. These means for manifesting acts of eternity are universal, in both the East and the West. Jesus Christ, Mother Teresa, and the great saints show what human beings can accomplish — that they can shine like the bright stars in the night sky. Nonetheless,

---

[1] See also James Martin, A Saint's Dark Night, *The New York Times*, August, 29, 2007.

[2] Recall we discussed *tonglen* in Ch. III, p. 60.

we do not have to live like saints to achieve important and significant things in our daily activities. We may be like mere, small candles, yet we can still bring light to our immediate surroundings.

Our daily activities have a very real impact on our own lives, as well as others. For example, people around us might be either agreeable and polite or disagreeable and impolite, depending on our own demeanors. Our own approach to life may subtly affect how those we contact respond to us. By being calm and peaceful, we perform our work more efficiently. Years ago, my family used to go to a local ice-skating ring. There were two workers who gave out rental skates and stored shoes for patrons. One worker was always smiling, and emanated his warmth to everyone who came to him. The other worker looked very testy, as if the job was being imposed upon her. Whenever possible, we would wait for the smiling worker to serve us. Who wouldn't?

Consider The Dalai Lama and how people enjoy his presence. This is simply because he exudes his compassion and joy. Those who are in his presence will be affected by his serenity and become calm and peaceful themselves. In fact his aura is so immense that he actually brightens the space around him. I was once in the audience of his public lecture in New York City's Central Park. I was so far away that I mainly listened and watched him on a big TV screen. Only now and then did I glance at him on the platform. At one point I noticed that the platform was flooded with a golden glow, which I had not observed before. I was absorbed in his talk and did not think too much about this observation. However, I later remembered I had once read that when The Dalai Lama comes into a room, he seems to bring light with him; the room will be brightened, but as soon as he leaves one feels that the room becomes darkened. He was most likely born with this aura, as he is now living his fourteenth incarnation as The Dalai Lama. Even so, he still works diligently to cultivate his inner balance. In *The Art of Happiness* [31, p. 225 and p. 298], he mentions that he does his daily meditation and prayer practice at half past three in the morning, sometimes for up to four hours.

We may not be able to practice meditation or prayer for as long. Even if we have the time and intent, we may not have developed sufficient perseverance to sit for such a long period. However, a habit of regular quiet contemplation will certainly enhance our well-being. We do not have to sit cross-legged or meditate by focusing on the breath. It may be enough just to put aside our usual routines and be quiet: either saying a prayer, or reading a classic spiritual text. The point is to focus our mind on some non-materialistic and non-urgent matter. Let us make that habit a sacred rite. According to the *more use, easier use* principle, once we have established a habit we can lengthen the duration of such contemplation and cultivate a steadier inner balance. As time progresses we may be amazed at the changes we experience. We may become less irritated over small inconveniences than before, or even able to laugh at ourselves every time we are about to lose our temper.

These changes will be subtle and gradual, as if we were an alchemist turning our drifting mind into the *golden elixir*. Let us study how the teachings of Taoist alchemy may benefit us. There are volumes of writings on the subject of alchemy.[3] I will only concentrate on a very limited but important aspect of alchemy that suits our modern perspective.

According to Taoism, the "one reality" spirit or energy that dwells in our human body splits into three parts.[4] Depending on their functions they are called:

---

[3]See, for example, *The Taoists Classics*, Vols. 2,3 [20] for a detailed exposition of the subject. The information here is gathered from those classics.

[4]See Ch. I, pp. 23–24, for a discussion of *the three meet*. Essentially, we are treating in this chapter the same subject matter in different terms.

(1) the *true intent*, which contains the impulse of life and directs our affairs,

(2) the *true sense of real knowledge*, or the *Tao mind*, which wards off external afflictions and stops internal aberrations, and

(3) the *true* or *spiritual essence of conscious knowledge*, or the *human mind*, which moves and harmonizes our living potential.

Attributes	Symbol I	Symbol II	Symbol III	Function
True Intent	Earth	Yellow Court	Center	Contains life impulse and directs affairs
True Sense (Tao mind, real knowledge, or true yang)	Lead	Golden Flower	White Tiger (Right side)	Wards off external afflictions and internal aberrations
True Essence (human mind, conscious knowledge or true yin)	Mercury	Flowing Pearl	Blue Dragon (Left side)	Harmonizes living potential

Table 2. The Three Attributes of One Reality

Since spirituality transcends our physical existence and is difficult to articulate for easy comprehension, Taoists employ a wide gamut of symbols and analogies to convey the principles of the alchemical science (see Table 2 and *The Inner Teaching of Taoism* [14] for a much longer list of symbols). For example, true intent is represented by the "earth," the "yellow court," and the "center" because it gives us life impulse and emanates from our center like the earth. True sense of real knowledge, the Tao mind, is represented by "lead," the "Golden Flower," [5] and the "white tiger" because it is heavy, illuminative, and strong.

---

[5] See also Ch. I, pp. 15–24 for discussions on the Golden Flower, which stands for the hidden Light.

The spiritual essence of conscious knowledge, the human mind, is represented by "mercury," the "flowing pearl," and the "blue dragon" because it is volatile and moves very rapidly. Moreover, the attributes of yin and yang and the symbols for WATER and FIRE (see Fig. 13) play very important roles in Taoist alchemy, and I will later investigate their attributes more fully.

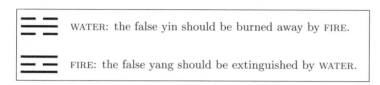

Figure 13. Trigrams WATER and FIRE.

The Tao mind is represented by yang. When yang functions properly with the right amount of "yang energy," it is firm and strong and is referred to as the *true yang*. When yang functions improperly with an excessive amount of yang energy, it is compulsive, aggressive and impatient, and is referred to as the *false yang*. The human mind is represented by yin. When yin functions properly with the right amount of "yin energy," it is flexible, open and courteous, and is referred to as the *true yin*. When yin functions improperly with an excess amount of yin energy, it is ineffective and vacillating and is referred to as the *false yin*. According to Taoist alchemy, the yang and yin energies in us are not always in the proper proportions, and act with a great deal of confusion (and not much coordination). This imbalance is explained in Taoism [14, p. 226]:

Once the real divides, the false comes forth; the seeds of routine take command, sense faculties and data stir together, and habit energy grows day by day: true intent becomes adulterated with artificial intentions, true sense becomes adulterated with arbitrary feelings, and spiritual essence becomes adulterated with temperament.

The falsehoods of yin and yang will confuse and mislead us. Spiritual alchemy hints at a process reuniting these three parts to return to "one reality" so that we no longer behave in a confused manner.

The primordial yang energy is represented by the trigram HEAVEN ☰ with three solid lines and the primordial yin by EARTH ☷ with three broken lines. But once they dwell in human beings, neither the three yang lines nor the three yin lines stay together. The yin and yang lines are shuffled — HEAVEN and EARTH change into the situations represented by the trigrams for WATER ☵ and FIRE ☲.

The trigram WATER ☵ has one solid yang line inside and two broken yin lines outside. This trigram is used as a symbol to represent our current state of real knowledge or the Tao mind. Real knowledge which is considered as true yang is now surrounded by acquired false yin influences. The true sense of our Tao mind cannot take control and hides inside acquired influences such as bad habits and selfish desires.

The trigram FIRE ☲ has one broken yin line inside and two solid yang lines outside. This trigram is used as a symbol to represent the state of conscious knowledge or the human mind. The spiritual essence of conscious knowledge, considered the true yin, is now affected by false yang temperaments or unbalanced emotions that easily flare up like fire. The spiritual essence of our human mind, which is supposed to be open and to submit to the true sense of the Tao mind, now tries to take control due to unbalanced emotions.

The change of the primordial energy to the states of WATER and FIRE is analogous to the idea of the Fall from Eden in the West. Loosely speaking, the Tao mind (real knowledge) may be regarded as our soul and the human mind (conscious knowledge) as our intellectual mind. The wife, Eve (conscious knowledge), is to follow the husband, Adam (real knowledge), as if the yin should let the yang take control. But when desires and conditioned habits take the lead, it is as if one follows the temptation of the outside (serpent) and so the calm and happiness of Eden is lost.

The difficulty in alchemy is *centering* [14, p. 227], the proper combination without imbalance of the essence of conscious knowledge with the sense of real knowledge. This centering mirrors what we discussed on inner balance earlier in the previous chapter. Alchemists suggest using true intent as the cauldron and furnace to coax FIRE and WATER to act on each other properly. FIRE should be placed underneath WATER. This way one can use FIRE to burn away the acquired influences (false yin) in WATER and use WATER to extinguish the unbalanced temperaments (false yang) in FIRE. When true yang and true yin emerge, they embrace like husband and wife and form the *spiritual embryo* or the golden elixir. After a period of incubation, a well developed spiritual infant will be born. What this signifies, to quote from the book *Practical Taoism* [15, p. 548], is that our "mind has no [more] attachments, myriad cogitations melt, and the basic spirit appears, coming and going freely, unobstructed by the physical body."

This teaching of alchemy is not so different from the doctrine of non-doing or *wu-wei*.[6] Taoists encourage students [14, p. 248] to continue this alchemical practice all the time

> ...to carry on the subtle path of non-doing. The child gives birth to grandchildren, and grandchildren also branch out, producing a thousand changes, ten thousand transformations. Each soars into the skies riding a crane, becoming immortals of the empyrean.

---

[6]See Ch. IV, pp. 73–75 for discussions of *wu-wei*.

I speculate that to give birth to these spiritual offspring is equivalent to what Jesus advises (*St. Matthew*, 6:20): "lay up for yourselves treasures in heaven."

Although real knowledge or true yang may be polluted by our acquired influences and bad habits, in fact it shows up frequently (however faintly) to guide us. Taoists apply the term *one yang arising* to signify this situation. It may be presumed that those who hear inner voices, realize their gut feelings, or experience moments of grace, do nurture the one yang arising. When we are calm and still, we may notice that true yang arises, too. In his book *Great Eastern Sun* [79, p. 21], Chögyam Trungpa Rinpoche, uses a "dot" in his teachings on the way of the warrior—the wisdom of *Shambhala*[7]—to symbolize our "primordial, unconditional, basic goodness." His emphasis on paying attention to the symbolic dot may also be viewed as observing the one yang arising.

The yang and yin energies keep waxing and waning all the time. Taoists use the solstices and equinoxes, times of the day, and phases of the moon to describe the energy states and advise practitioners how to act accordingly. The Taoist expert Liu I-Ming explains in *The Inner Teachings of Taoism* [14, p. 239] that one yang arises, for example, during the winter solstice or at midnight. When it does, "one should quickly advance the fire and gather it, assisting this bit of faint yang to gradually grow and develop, not letting it fade away." On the other hand, a point of yin energy comes during summer solstice or at midday. When it comes, "one should quickly work to repel it, suppressing this bit of false yin, evaporating it as it grows, not letting up for a moment." During the spring and autumn equinoxes or at 6 a. m. and 6 p. m., yin and yang are "at midway between heaven and earth," like the half moon with equal amounts of darkness and

---

[7]*Shambhala* is a Sanskrit term meaning "place of peace, tranquility, and happiness." Trungpa, the great Tibetan Buddhist, is the founder of *Shambhala* Training.

brightness, and these are appropriate times to combine firmness with flexibility in a harmonious manner.

Some practitioners apply these teachings and can "prolong life, see forever, and not die." [8] "In reality," says one master [15, p. 548], such "transcendent liberation ... is just a matter of temporarily using refinement of vitality and refinement of energy to focus the mind and nurture the basic spirit so that it is effective." The purpose of these teachings is to help us endow our mundane daily activities with an eternal status. By the *as above, so below* principle, we may consider the start of each breath or activity as one yang arising. Then we calm our fleeting mind, quiet down our myriad of inner desires, and center our inner balance. We can totally dedicate ourselves to the task at hand with firmness, focus, and without selfish desires, as well as with sincerity, humility, and without emotional attachments. Thus yang and yin both function properly and the completion of a task is equivalent to the creation of an everlasting aura brightening our spiritual world.

By the *more use, easier use* principle we can eventually complete all our tasks with this attitude and form a whole family of spiritual offspring. We may imagine that we are developing a spiritual Sierpinski's triangle. Each point in the triangle represents the spiritual child of an alchemical accomplishment. The result is *the three meet*—the harmony of our true intent, true yang and true yin. Many of us have neither been able to crystallize the golden elixir, nor to incubate the spiritual embryo to full term. The points of our spiritual Sierpinski's triangle are few and sparse.

Why is it that masters (such as Confucius) can be peaceful and detached even in the face of calamity, but few of us can? Perhaps they understand the Way and have practiced diligently.

---

[8]See [15, p. 514]. For example, Lu Tung-pin is one such immortal in the Taoist legend.

There is no shortcut from learning to gaining results in the practice of Tao.

Let me use the study of Mathematics to draw an analogy regarding why diligent practice is important. When presented with a math problem, many students simply apply random operations on the numbers and may turn an easy problem into a very complicated puzzle. Those who have studied and done their homework exercises need only to try a few familiar methods before they will be able to derive the solution step by step. On the other hand, the teacher can visualize those few steps that will lead to the answer and may even see the answer instantly. In fact, in solving math problems any student can become as proficient as the teacher if they are willing to study and practice what they have been taught.

When people (even masters) encounter an unexpected calamity, their first reaction is "why me" or "why this." Such emotions prevent ordinary people from finding an efficient way to deal with the situation. The masters, however, with their industrious practice, are able to expedite the passage from encountering a problem (and to ignore the "why" phase) to arrive at a solution in an easy manner. The majority of us are trapped in the "why" phase because we have not practiced sufficiently to calm our mind. When we practice meditation, we are cultivating our ability to move inside and sink deeper and deeper into our inexhaustible Godhead. When we interact with others, it is like going outside and radiating what we have from deep inside us. The deeper and more penetratingly we delve inside, the brighter and broader we radiate when we go outside.

The Tao is in everything and in every activity, waiting for us to discern it. If we calm our mind of all its ideas and desires, we will become closer to the Tao. The book *Awakening to the Tao* [17] is a compilation of contemplations by the Taoist expert Liu I-Ming. Among other things, he shows us how simple objects and events can reveal the deep aspects of the Tao. Readers will find in this wonderful book inspirations to nurture a fresh and tranquil relationship with their surroundings and with themselves.

There is an inspiring story about a butcher [88, pp. 50–51].

> Once a butcher cut up an ox in front of a king. He was very skillful and every cut was made effortlessly and precisely at the joints. The king was intrigued by his dexterity. This butcher told the king that usually a novice butcher has to sharpen his cleaver every month and an expert, every year. Yet he had been carving oxen for nineteen years without ever blunting his cleaver. He explained, "I was actually practicing the Tao while carving. When I was a novice, I could only see the whole ox. After three years I no longer saw the ox as a whole. Now I do not need to look at the ox and can just let my true intent guide my cleaver to the joints."
>
> —abstracted from *Chuang Tzu*, Ch. 3

Every task and every situation in our lives provide us with an opportunity to practice the Tao. Meditation is only one such activity. Poetry appreciation is another activity that is particularly rich in spiritual nourishment. We can learn from poets how they transcend their feelings and emotions. Dr. Elisabeth Kübler-Ross, a psychiatrist with expertise on death and dying, reports in her book *The Wheel of Life: A Memoir of Living and Dying* [38, pp. 217–223] that she once experienced a state of Cosmic Consciousness. She wondered why she could have such an experience, since she never practiced meditation. Someone pointed out to her that her total dedication to her patients and her willingness to sit with them compassionately for hours before their death was no different from practicing meditation.

Even very mundane tasks bring us enlightenment. There is an inspiring story about Ksudrapanthaka, one of Buddha's early disciples. He was so dumb that he could not even remember his own name. The only job he could do was to sweep floors. Buddha taught him to concentrate on the broom while he swept. It was reported that he was thus enlightened. So indeed, every activity invites us to discover the Tao.

In *Metamorphoses* [49, Bk. XI, **Midas and the golden touch**] by the Roman poet Ovid, King Midas wished everything that he touched would turn into gold. His wish was granted by the wine god Bacchus. However, when he found out that he could neither eat nor drink with such a golden touch, he asked Bacchus to forgive his sin and take away this power.

There are different lessons to be learned from this story. I would interpret the "golden touch" spiritually as the *means* to bestow on our activities an eternal status. Our work, words, and virtues are our means to touch others. In order to transform our activities to the "golden elixir," it is important that we do not let greed and selfish desires obscure our true sense and essence like Midas did. Of course, this is an ideal that cannot be accomplished in a short time. But a journey of ten thousand miles starts with one step. If we never take the first step we will never get anywhere. Let us see how long it took Confucius to be one with Tao.

> At fifteen I set my heart on learning.
> At thirty I stood firmly.
> At forty I was free of doubts.
> At fifty I understood the Decree of Heaven.
> At sixty my ears were attuned.
> At seventy I could follow and please my heart
> Without trespassing outside the square.
>
> — *The Analects*, Bk. II:4

At the tender age of fifteen, Confucius decided to learn how to be a true human being. He studied poetry, history, music, rituals, and divination. At thirty, his study led him to affirm his stand to follow the Tao. Then, it took him ten more years till age forty to arrive at the stage of not being confused or disturbed by external events. At fifty he understood the mystery of the universe and the relation between man and Heaven.[9]

Confucius approached his learning objectively and earnestly, with humility throughout his life. It was reported that when he entered the royal temple he inquired about and adhered to every rite. This event took place when he was in his fifties, and at that time he was already a famous teacher well respected by his contemporaries. According to another story (see Ch. V, p. 93), he was thankful for his misfortunes, which he considered as opportunities to strengthen his virtues. Both stories show his humble attitude toward learning.

He attained complete harmony at age sixty. Nothing he heard would be offending to his ears. How often do people hear criticisms from others and consider them music to their ears? Most frequently, they would feel irritated and rebut immediately. It does take a tremendous amount of inner work to train oneself to be free of likes or dislikes and regard any comments by others simply as expressions of *their* state of mind. Confucius told us that he achieved the "ears attuned" stage only at age sixty, forty-five years after he first made up his mind to study, when he was fifteen.

When we have our "ears attuned" we will listen to whatever is said without judgment. After reaching this state, it is natural to advance to the state of complete self-control. Confucius told us that he had to work diligently for ten more years to reach

---

[9]It was most likely during this period that he articulated the ideas of and reportedly wrote the ten commentaries on the classic *I-Ching*.

that stage. He was finally totally anchored to his center with perfect inner balance and without deviating from the Way, that is, without trespassing outside the square. [10] Recall the symbol ⊡ of the square inside the circle by the Taoist Liu I-Ming in Ch. VI (p. 105). Most likely this statement of Confucius inspired Liu to make that icon since Liu was a Confucian scholar before becoming a Taoist. The symbol represents an ideal of conduct and Confucius told us he accomplished that at seventy. We may infer that Confucius was one with Tao — inside he was stable without any aberration, like a square, and outside he responded to people harmoniously and evenly, like a circle.

Confucius passed away at seventy-two or seventy-three. He most likely only commented about his progress in his very late years. Like J. J. Lynn (Rajasi Janakananda), Mother Teresa, and Thomas Merton in modern times, Confucius also disappeared after he had completed his task of showing a path for Self-realization.

We may not be as holy as Confucius or Mother Teresa, but we can be courteous and warm like the smiling worker at the skating rink. Let me relate a true story about a moderately well-to-do merchant on a small island. In his old age this merchant had trouble walking and needed someone to carry him between his home and his shop. Part of the street was in need of repair but the government had not allocated any funds for resurfacing. The old man donated money to have that part of the road resurfaced. Neighbors came to thank him and said that they would never be rich enough to carry out a charitable work of such a magnitude. The old man consoled them, "If you see a banana peel on the

---

[10]The Chinese original of my translation "square" is 矩, which is usually translated as "rule," or "law." However, there is no fixed rule on how to follow the Tao, so we should not say Confucius follows a rule. He simply does whatever his heart urges him to do. Since 矩 also means a square (or rectangle), we interpret the text to mean that whatever Confucius does agrees with the Way because he has achieved complete stillness inside. See also Ch. V, pp. 83–86 on stillness.

street and pick it up, that is no less charitable than fixing bridges
or resurfacing roads." Really, there is no need to compare acts
of compassion. They are all meritorious.

We frequently have to work by ourselves. We may feel that
our work has no impact whatsoever, or that no one ever notices
what we do. However, these are in fact illusions. Just like the
sun is always there, Intelligence is always with us. Our work is
like a solitary orchid growing in a spacious valley. The orchid
will bloom and manifest its beauty and fragrance whether it is
appreciated or not. The lotus root is embedded in mud and
yet its flower emerges with complete purity. Our work does not
need to be a showy flower. In *The Story of A Soul* [75, pp. 2–3],
St. Therese of Lisieux (1873–1897) observes that, "The brilliance
of the rose and the whiteness of the lily don't take away the
perfume of the lovely violet or the delightful simplicity of the
daisy." She teaches us that every little flower encompasses
the purity and elegance of its transcendence. With sincerity,
humility, and detachment from personal rewards we can become
a real alchemist, transforming the mundane into celestial gold,
forever and ever.

IX

Amen

We have come to the end of our exploration of *The Lord's Prayer*. As is to be expected, people from different cultural traditions may view *The Lord's Prayer* in quite different ways. Contemplative praying is a private activity during which we engage in a personal dialogue with our Father. Here is a version of my contemplation.

Our Father, our Mother, and our Great Tao, You are pure Consciousness in a state of infinite compassion and eternal bliss. *As above, so below,* we can also attain such a state. We only have to seek the "I AM" within and bring out our highest ideals. All our activities are subject to the *more use, easier use* principle. We know that "practice makes perfect" but we need to be careful so as to not be entrapped by our undesirable habits.

Thy kingdom as the Christ Consciousness is inherent in the virtues of compassion, courage, humility, and patience. Holy Mary, help us birth the Christ within. Oh Father! Inspire us to emulate Heaven and Earth: creating yet without possessing so that we can complete our will with *wu-wei* and acquire less *action-reaction* karma.

We are grateful that our daily bread is given like air is given. We only have to perform our tasks the same way we breathe. If we worry and *persist* in asking for something, then that something may continue to *resist* appearing. The practice of becoming adept at activating the mind without dwelling on any thought will ease our worry and expedite our work.

When we interact with others, conflicts are sometimes unavoidable. Help us understand that hate and unforgiving attitudes only hurt us even more, and forgiving others is really for our own well-being. Encourage us to assist others to accomplish that to which we also aspire and avoid imposing on others what we don't desire.

Thou has sent great teachers to show us how to harmonize our inner urges with our outer behaviors. Lead us to follow Christ Jesus and practice the middle way, balancing our material and spiritual activity. With sincerity, humility, and detachment from personal rewards, we can become true alchemists, transforming the mundane into celestial gold forever and ever.

AMEN.

Appendix

A Brief Description of Iterated Function Systems

In mathematics, a *function* is a rule or formula to compute a new number from a given number. For example, if the formula is $x + 1$, then given any number x, the function computes a new number by adding 1 to it. So given $x = 3$, the function will compute $3 + 1 = 4$. We say that the function *maps* the number 3 *to* the number 4, and more generally, the function *maps* a given number x *to* the number $x + 1$. If we change the formula to say $x + 2$, then we obtain a new function that computes a new number by adding 2 to the input.

To allow for similar functions but with different addends, we can denote a family of functions by a more general formula $x + \lambda$ where x is still the given number, but λ is a *parameter*. If the parameter $\lambda = 1$, we obtain the first example function above and if the parameter $\lambda = 2$, we obtain the second example function.

We say the formula $x + \lambda$ is *parameterized* with parameter λ. A formula may have more than one parameter, for example the formula $kx + \lambda$ has two parameters k and λ. A *function system* is a parameterized mathematical formula representing a family (or system) of functions when the parameters vary. We use a pair of braces around a formula with parameters to denote a *function system*, like $\{kx + \lambda\}$.

By *iterations* we mean repeatedly evaluating a function at a formerly evaluated value or initial value. If the function is $x + 1$, and we start with $x = 3$, we first compute the value 4 as before, and we can compute the next iteration by adding 1 to the result to get 5. Repeating the iteration again, we next get 6 and then 7, and so on. The set of values (or points) obtained by iteration based on some starting value is called an *orbit*. The orbit for our example starting from 3 is $3, 4, 5, 6, 7, \ldots$. If we had started from 14, the orbit would have been $14, 15, 16, 17, 18, \ldots$.

A system of functions together with their iterations (or orbits) is called an *Iterated Function System* (IFS).

Let us look at the simple family of functions $\{kx\}$. Here k is the parameter and x is the input. For each parametric value k, there corresponds a function that maps x to the value kx.

(i) If k is 1 then the function will be an identity function with formula x and will map every value x to itself. For this function, the orbit of every point will be the point itself.

(ii) If k is 2, then the function $2x$ will multiply every value of x by 2. For this function the orbit of the number 0 will be 0. The orbit of the number 1 will be the sequence: $1, 2, 4, 8, 16$ and so on. This sequence will eventually escape to infinity or be *unbounded*.

(iii) If k is $\frac{1}{2}$, then the function $\frac{x}{2}$ will divide the value x by 2. For this function, the orbit of the number 0 will be 0. The orbit of the number 1 will be the sequence: $1, \frac{1}{2}, \frac{1}{4}, \frac{1}{8}, \frac{1}{16}, \ldots$. The sequence will eventually converge to 0 and in particular is bounded.

(iv) If k is -1, then the function $-x$ will change the sign of the value x. For this function, the orbit of the number 0 will be 0. The orbit of the number 1 will be the sequence: $1, -1, 1, -1, \ldots$. The sequence will neither converge nor escape to infinity, but it is bounded.

So we see that for a function in the system, its orbits may be bounded or unbounded. Points of bounded orbits are of particular interest in Chaos Theory.

Let us consider another system $\{z^2 - \lambda\}$ where λ is the parameter and z is the variable. Here both λ and z are *complex numbers* which can be identified with points on the plane. For our purpose, it is enough to know that points on the plane can be multiplied and added to give other points on the plane. For each (parameter) point λ on the plane, there corresponds a function that maps a point z to the point $z^2 - \lambda$.

For each function (or parameter) in this system the set of points with bounded orbits (that is, all the points in the orbit lie within some big circle) is called a *filled Julia set* and its boundary is called a *Julia set*. The term "Julia set" is sometimes relaxed to mean the filled Julia set. Different parameters would give rise to different functions and Julia sets of different shapes and connectedness.

Loosely speaking, a *Mandelbrot set* is the set of parameters for which the corresponding functions have connected Julia sets. A Mandelbrot set plays somewhat the role of a pictorial guide in the parameter space revealing the feature of its associated Julia sets. In Chaos Theory, this IFS has been investigated in great detail and its computer-generated graphical representations are used as a model for certain fractal nature of Tao in this book.

Please refer to Fig. 10 of Ch. I (p. 40) for an illustration of
the Mandelbrot and Julia sets of this IFS, which is taken from
Barnsley [2] where more illustrations and detailed presentations
of Chaos Theory are given.   For different IFS with similar
functions the associated MJS may look very different from
that shown in Fig. 10, yet these intrinsic characteristics remain
unchanged. We show here Fig. 14, which is the graphics for the
MJS of another IFS for comparison. You may have to inspect
more closely to locate the positions for the pairs of corresponding
Julia sets.

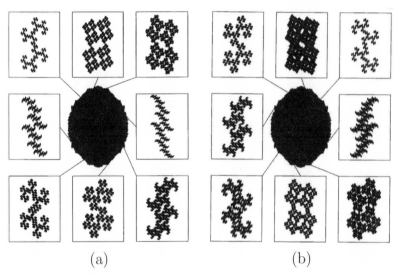

(a)   (b)

Figure 14.   (a) Some of the fractals to be found at various points
near the boundary of the Mandelbrot set associated with the
parametrized family of IFS $\{\mathbb{C}; \lambda z - 1, \lambda z + 1\}$. (b) Same as (a). Where
would you look for an interesting fractal? Reproduced by permission from
Michael Barnsley, *Fractals Everywhere* [2, Fig. 8.2.5].

For an interactive illustration of fractal features of the
Mandelbrot and Julia sets, you can also visit the website created
by Robert Devaney: `http://www.ibiblio.org/e-notes/MSet`
`/Anim/ManJuOrb.htm`.

Bibliography

1. Alighieri, Dante. *Purgatorio*, trans. by W. S. Merwin, Alfred A. Knopf, New York, 2000.
2. Barnsley, Michael. *Fractals Everywhere*, Academy Press, New York, 1988.
3. Benson, Herbert. *The Relaxation Response*, K. G. Hall, Boston, 1976.
4. Campbell, Dan. *Edgar Cayce on the Power of Colors, Stones, and Crystals*, Charles T. Cayce, ed., Warner Book, New York, 1989.
5. Campbell, Joseph. *The Hero with a Thousand Faces*, Commemorative Ed., Princeton University Press, Princeton, 2004.
6. Carter, Jimmy. *Our Endangered Values: America's Moral Crisis*, Simon & Schuster, New York, 2005.
7. Chödrön, Pema. *The Wisdom of No Escape and the Path of Loving-Kindness*, Shambhala, Boston, 1991.
8. Cleary, Thomas, trans. *The Flower Ornament Scripture*, Shambhala, Boston, 1993.
9. _____, trans. *Buddhist Yoga: A Comprehensive Course*, Shambhala, Boston, 1995.
10. _____, trans. *Minding Mind: A Course in Basic Meditation*, Shambhala, Boston, 1995.
11. _____, trans. *The Sutra of Hui-neng: Grand Master of Zen*, with Hui-neng's Commentary on the Diamond Sutra, Shambhala, Boston, 1998.
12. _____. *The Taoist Classics: The Collected Translations of Thomas Cleary*, Vol. 1, *Wen Tzu*, Shambhala, Boston, 1999.
13. _____. *The Taoist Classics: The Collected Translations of Thomas Cleary*, Vol. 2, *Understanding Reality*, Shambhala, Boston, 1999.
14. _____. *The Taoist Classics: The Collected Translations of Thomas Cleary*, Vol. 2, *The Inner Teaching of Taoism*, Shambhala, Boston, 1999.
15. _____. *The Taoist Classics: The Collected Translations of Thomas Cleary*, Vol. 2, *Practical Taoism*, Shambhala, Boston, 1999.
16. _____. *The Taoist Classics: The Collected Translations of Thomas Cleary*, Vol. 3, *The Secrets of the Golden Flower*, Shambhala, Boston, 1999.
17. _____. *The Taoist Classics: The Collected Translations of Thomas Cleary*, Vol. 3, *Awakening to the Tao*, Shambhala, Boston, 1999.
18. _____. *The Taoist Classics: The Collected Translations of Thomas Cleary*, Vol. 3, *Vitality, Energy, Spirit: A Taoist Sourcebook*, Shambhala, Boston, 1999.
19. _____. *The Taoist Classics: The Collected Translations of Thomas Cleary*, Vol. 4, *The Taoist I-Ching*, Shambhala, Boston, 1999.
20. _____. *The Taoist Classics: The Collected Translations of Thomas Cleary*, Vols. 1,2,3,4, Shambhala, Boston, 2003.

21. Du Boulay, Shirley. *Teresa of Avila: An Extraordinary Life*, BlueBridge, New York, 2004.
22. Durga, Mata. *A Paramhansa Yogananda Trilogy of Divine Love*, J. Wight Pub., Beverley Hills, CA, 1993.
23. Dyer, Wayne W., *There is a Spiritual Solution to Every Problem*, Harper-Collins Pubs., New York, 2001.
24. Easwaran, Eknath, trans. *The Bhagavad Gita*, Nilgiri Press, Tomales, CA, 1985.
25. Feild, Reshad. *The Last Barrier: A Journey into the Essence of Sufi Teachings*, 25th anniv. ed., Lindisfarne Books, Great Barrington, MA, 2002.
26. Gladwell, Malcolm. *Blink: The Power of Thinking without Thinking*, Little Brown & Company, New York, 2005.
27. Greene, Brian. *The Elegant Universe*, Vantage Books, New York, 2000.
28. Gyatso, Tenzin (The Dalai Lama). *An Open Heart: Practicing Compassion in Everyday Life*, Nicolas Vreeland, ed., Little Brown, Boston, 2001.
29. _____. *The Universe in a Single Atom*, Morgan Road Books, New York, 2005.
30. _____. *The Essence of the Heart Sutra*, trans. & ed. by Geshe Thupten Jinpa, Wisdom Publ., Boston, 2005.
31. Gyatso, Tenzin (The Dalai Lama) and Cutler, Howard C. M. D. *The Art of Happiness*, Riverhead Books, New York, 1998.
32. Harvey, Andrew. *The Son of Man*, J. P. Tarcher/Putnam, New York, 1998.
33. _____. *Sun at Midnight: A Memoir of the Dark Night*, J. P. Tarcher/Putnam, New York, 2002.
34. Hayward, Jeremy W. and Varela, Francisco J. *Gentle Bridges: Conversations with The Dalai Lama on the Sciences of Mind*, Shambhala, Boston, 1992.
35. Jampolsky, Gerald G. *Love Is Letting Go of Fear*, Celestial Arts, Millbrae, CA, 1979.
36. _____. *One Person Can Make a Difference: Ordinary People Doing Extraordinary Things*. Bantam Books, New York, 1990.
37. Jiang, K. J., Deng, L., and Payne, M. G. Superluminal propagation of an optical pulse in a Doppler-broadened three-state single-channel active Raman gain medium, *Phys. Rev. A*, **76** (2007), 033819 (4 pages).
38. Kübler-Ross, Elisabeth. *The Wheel of Life: A Memoir of Living and Dying*, Scriber, New York, 1997.
39. _____. *On Life after Death*, Celestial Arts, Berkeley, 1991.
40. Merton, Thomas. *The Seven Storey Mountain*, Harcourt Brace & Company, New York, 1978, ©1948.
41. _____. *New Seeds on Contemplation*, New Directions, New York, 1961.
42. _____. *The Asian Journal of Thomas Merton*, Burton, N., Br. Hart, P., & Laughlin, J., eds., New Directions, New York, 1975.
43. _____. *A Search for Solitude: Pursuing the Monk's True Life*, HarperSanFrancisco, San Francisco, 1996.
44. _____. *The Other Side of the Mountain*, HarperSanFrancisco, San Francisco, 1998.

45. _____. *The Inner Experience*: *Notes on Contemplation*, HarperSanFrancisco, San Francisco, 2003.

46. M. (Mahendranath Gupta). *The Gospel of Sri Ramakrishna*, trans. by Nikhilananda, Swami. Ramakrishna-Vivekananda Center, New York, 1942.

47. Nyana, Bhikku (Mahathera Ledi Sayadaw). *The Vipassana Dipani; Or the Manual of Insight*, trans. by Sayadaw U. Nyana, AMS Press, Inc., New York, 1988. On-line version: `http://www.ubakhin.com/ledi/MANUAL01.html`.

48. Ouspensky, P. D. *In Search of the Miraculous*, Harcourt, San Diego, 2001.

49. Ovid, *Metamorphoses*, trans. by Rolfe Humphries, Indiana Univ. Press, Bloomington, 1983.

50. Palmer, Martin. *The Jesus Sutras*: *Rediscovering the Lost Religion of Taoist Christianity*, Ballantine, New York, 2001.

51. Patrul, Rinpoche. *The Words of My Perfect Teacher*, trans. by the Padmakara Translation Group, Rev. Ed., Shambhala, Boston, 1998.

52. Peck, M. Scott. *Further Along the Road Less Traveled*: *The Unending Journey Toward Spiritual Growth*, Simon & Schuster, New York, 1993.

53. Plato. *Collected Dialogues*, Hamilton, E. & Cairns, H. (eds.), Princeton Univ. Press, Princeton, 1961.

54. Powell, Robert A. *The Most Holy Trinosophia*: *The New Revelation of the Divine Feminine*, Anthroposophic Press, Great Barrington, MA, 2000.

55. Robinovitz, Karen. JOURNEYS; No Talking. No Fun. It's Called A Vacation, Travel Section, *The New York Times*, Jan. 16, 2004.

56. Rubinstein, Artur. *My Young Years*, Knopf, New York, 1973.

57. _____. *My Many Years*, Knopf, New York, 1980.

58. Sheldrake, Rupert. *A New Science of Life*, Revised & Expanded, J. P. Tarcher, Los Angeles, 1981.

59. _____. *The Presence of the Past*, Times Books, Random House, Inc., New York, 1988.

60. Smith, Edward Reaugh. *The Burning Bush*, Anthroposophic Press, New York, 2001.

61. _____. *David's Question*: *"What is Man?"* Anthroposophic Press, New York, 2003.

62. _____. *The Soul's Long Journey*: *How the Bible Reveals Reincarnation*, SteinerBooks, Great Barrington, MA., 2003.

63. Steiner, Rudolf. *Karma*, Anthroposophic Press, New York, 1943.

64. _____. *Life Between Death and Rebirth*, Anthroposophic Press, New York, 1968.

65. _____. *Esoteric Development*, Anthroposophic Press, Spring Valley, NY, 1982.

66. _____. *The Influences of Lucifer & Ahriman*, Anthroposophic Press, Hudson, NY, 1993.

67. _____. *How to Know Higher Worlds*, Anthroposophic Press, Great Barrington, MA., 1994.

68. _____. *The Fifth Gospel*: *From the Akashic Record*, Rudolf Steiner Press, East Sussex, 1995.

69. _____. *Autobiography*, SteinerBooks, Great Barrington, MA, 2006.

70. Sugrue, Thomas. *There is a River: The Story of Edgar Cayce*, A. R. E. Press, Virginia Beach, 1997.

71. Teresa of Avila. *The Life of Teresa of Jesus*, Image Books, Garden City, NY, 1960.

72. _____. *The Way of Perfection*, Paraclete Press, Brewster, MA, 2000.

73. Teresa, Mother. *In the Heart of the World: Thoughts, Stories, and Prayers*, New World Library, Novato, CA, 1997.

74. _____. *Come Be My Light: The Private Writings of the Saint of Calcutta*, with Commentary by Brian Kolodiejchuk, M. C. (ed.), Doubleday, New York, 2007.

75. Therese of Lisieux. *The Story of a Soul*, Robert J. Edmonson, trans. & ed., Paraclete Press, Brewster, MA, 2006.

76. Thomas, Aquinas. *The Shorter Summa*, Sophia Institute Press, Manchester, NH, 2002.

77. Thoreau, Henry David. *Walden*, Shambhala, Boston, 2004.

78. Trungpa, Chögyam. *Born In Tibet*, Harcourt, Brace & World, New York, 1968.

79. _____. *Great Eastern Sun: The Wisdom of Shambhala*, Shambhala, Boston, 2001.

80. _____. *Mudra: Early Poems & Songs*, Shambhala, Boston, 2001.

81. _____. *Training the Mind and Cultivating Loving-Kindness*, Judith L. Lief, ed., Shambhala, Boston, 2003.

82. Vrekhem, Georges Van. *Beyond the Human Species: The Life and Work of Sri Aurobindo and The Mother*, Paragon House, St. Paul, 1998.

83. Wachsmuth, Guenther. *The Life and Work of Rudolf Steiner*, Whittier Books, New York, 1955.

84. Walsch, Neale Donald. *Conversations with God: an Uncommon Dialogue*, (Book 1), G. P. Putnam's Sons, New York, 1995.

85. _____. *Conversations with God: an Uncommon Dialogue*, (Book 2), Hampton Roads Pub. Co. Inc., Charlottesville, VA, 1997.

86. _____. *Conversations with God: an Uncommon Dialogue*, (Book 3), Hampton Roads, Pub. Co. Inc., Charlottesville, VA, 1998.

87. Wang L. J., Kuzmich, A., and Dogariu, A. Gain-assisted superluminal light propagation, *Nature*, **406** (July 20, 2000), 277–279.

88. Watson, Burton, trans. *The Complete Works of Chuang Tzu*, Columbia Univ. Press, New York, 1968.

89. Wilhelm, Richard, trans. *The Secret of the Golden Flower*, Harcourt Brace & Co., New York, 1962.

90. Yogananda, Paramhansa. *The Rubaiyat of Omar Khayyam Explained*, Walters, J. Donald (Swami Kriyananda), ed., Crystal Clarity Publishers, Nevada City, CA, 1994.

91. _____. *The Autobiography of a Yogi*, Self-Realization Fellowship, Los Angeles, 2000.

92. Zajonc, Arthur. *Catching the Light*, Bantam Books, New York, 1993.

Index